Nigel Cawthorne is the author of more than two hundred
books and is thought to be the

i.. London.

The Curious Cures of Old England

NIGEL CAWTHORNE

ROBINSON

ROBINSON

First published in Great Britain in 2005 by Portrait, an imprint of Piatkus

This paperback edition published in 2018 by Robinson

1 3 5 7 9 10 8 6 4 2

A CIP catalogue record for this book
is available from the British Library.

ISBN 978-1-472-14245-0

Printed and bound in Great Britain by CPI Group (UK) Ltd, Croydon, CR0 4YY

Papers used by Robinson are from well-managed forests and
other responsible sources.

Robinson
An imprint of
Little, Brown Book Group
Carmelite House
50 Victoria Embankment
London EC4Y 0DZ

An Hachette UK Company
www.hachette.co.uk

www.littlebrown.co.uk

Contents

Introduction

N OLD ENGLAND THERE were odd ailments whose cures seem curious to us today. That does not mean they did not work. A lot of modern-day medical cures started out as folk remedies. The leaves of several evergreen plants often prescribed by medieval herbalists contain salicylic acid, the principal ingredient of aspirin. Quinine, effective against malaria and other fevers, comes from the bark of the cinchona tree. This bark – originally called Peruvian or Jesuit's bark – was known to be effective against fever long before the active ingredient was isolated. Many other old herbal remedies have found their way, in chemical form, into the modern pharmacopoeia.

Before the modern scientific age, doctors had little to go on. They used ancient books and proceeded by trial and error – the error often resulting in the death of the patient. Doctors and surgeons had little idea about how the human body worked, because until the Renaissance no one cut up dead bodies to study anatomy. The practice was banned by numerous popes and forbidden by the Koran.

Until the seventeenth century most knowledge of anatomy came from the work of the Greek writer Galen of Pergamon, who lived in first-century Anatolia, Turkey. He cut up monkeys, pigs, sheep and goats, although he got a clearer idea of how the human body worked from his involvement in the treatment of wounded gladiators.

One twelfth-century physician maintained that 'the stomach has the liver below it like a fire underneath a cauldron; and thus is like a kettle of food, the gall bladder its cook, and the liver is the fire'. The colon was thought to be a sieve that strained faeces. Generally, the stomach was thought to be a cold, dry organ that served as a crossroads for all the arteries and veins. As it was constantly churning and generating waste products, it was located at the lower end of the torso, well away from the 'higher' organs. Respiration was thought to take place in the intestines, with waste gases being passed to the lungs, which exhaled them.

In the Dark Ages, systematic medical knowledge was confined to religious establishments that could care for the sick and dying. However, the Council of Tours in 1169 and the bull *Ecclesia Abhorret a Sanguine* (The Church Abhors Bloodshed), issued by Pope Innocent III in 1215, forbade priests and monks from spilling blood, which is why they burned witches and heretics. Their surgical knowledge was passed to the barbers, who came to the monasteries to attend to their tonsures and

trim their beards. Although barbers were men who knew how to wield sharp instruments, they were looked down on by doctors who knew about herbs and medicines – which is why surgeons are still called 'Mr' rather than 'Dr'.

Even when Leonardo da Vinci and other Renaissance figure started cutting up people, medical knowledge did not seem to increase very much. The function of the thyroid gland, for example, remained a puzzle. In the seventeenth century it was considered that its main purpose was to enhance women's beauty by filling out their necks.

Anatomists were also unable to locate the '*luz*', or '*neskvi*' – a cubic bone about the size of a barley corn the Hebrew Talmud said was to be found at the top of the spine, under the brain, hidden under a web of spider-like blood vessels. It was nourished only by the food eaten on Saturday night at the *melave malka* meal. The *luz* was thought to be indestructible. Apparently the Roman Emperor Hadrian tried to dissolve it, burn it and grind it – all to no avail. When he tried to crush it with a hammer, both the hammer and the anvil it was sitting on broke.

The other great mystery of anatomical science was the whereabouts of the soul. Although anatomists could not find it, they thought that it could be dislodged and escape when you sneezed. This is, perhaps, the origin of the habit of saying 'Bless you' when someone sneezes.

While monks could not work as surgeons, they could be physicians. Monasteries cultivated herb gardens and, as cities grew up, their products were sold through apothecaries. As trade spread, apothecaries began selling products from abroad, which arrived in England with extravagant claims about their healing properties. Doctors did what they could with these herbs and drugs, along with traditional folk remedies.

It is easy to ridicule old England's medical men, but they did their best and sometimes their cures proved effective – even if it was due to the placebo effect. Doctors today still prescribe harmless placebos, knowing that if the patient believes something is going to help their condition, it may well do so.

In the seventeenth and eighteenth centuries, as medical science developed, there was a struggle between those who adopted the new scientific approach and those who stuck to older, shall we say, more intuitive methods. The scientific men dismissed the others as 'quacks' – a word that came into the language in 1638, according to *Webster's Dictionary*. The first citation in the *Oxford English Dictionary* comes from 1659. Quack is an abbreviation of 'quacksalver' (first citation 1579), which is thought to derive from the old Dutch word *Kwabzalver* – *kwab* means a wen or cyst and *zalver* an ointment. Other authorities say that it derives from *Quecksilber*, the German for quicksilver, or mercury, which was often prescribed. Like most poisons, mercury does have a curative effect. While it is poisoning you, it also poisons the bacteria and viruses that are attacking you.

It is true that there were a number of out-and-out charlatans and mountebanks around in the seventeenth and eighteenth centuries. However, not all practitioners condemned as quacks were shysters. Many were simply peddling the old cures that were being challenged by the new medical establishment.

It should be remembered that a number of eminent medical men also lent their names to what we might now consider quack remedies. Sir Richard Mead (1673–1754) was the leading doctor of his day. He was royal physician to Queen Anne, George I and George II, and attended Isaac Newton, Alexander Pope and Prime Minister Robert Walpole. He also had a few curious cures up his voluminous sleeve. He prescribed a secret powder that would cure the bite of a mad dog. Serum treatment for rabies was only introduced in 1899. Otherwise rabies is fatal, although there was one case of recovery without serum treatment in 1971.

At the age of 29, in 1702, Mead published the ground-breaking scientific work *A Mechanical Account of Poisons*. In it, he described the effects of the tarantula bite:

Although the pain of its bite is at first no greater, than what is caused by the sting of a bee; yet the … patient within a few hours is seized with a violent sickness, … [and] in a short time expires; unless music be called to his assistance, which alone, without the help of medicine, performs the cure. For at the first sound of the musical instrument, although the sick lie, as it were, in an apoplectic fit, they begin by degrees to move their hands and feet; till at last they get up, and fall to dancing with wonderful vigour. At this sport they usually spend twelve hours a day, and it continues three or four days; by which time they are generally freed from all their symptoms.

As the master of the Royal College of Surgeons, Sir Charles Blicke (1745–1815) used 'Plunket's Caustic' as a cancer cure. It was made from 'crowsfoot, dog fennel, crude brimstone each of three middling thimblefuls and white arsenic the same quantity'. The recipe went on: 'Beat well and mix in a mortar, and make into small balls the size of nutmegs, and dry in the sun.' Although it probably would not have killed the patient – not right away, at least – it would certainly not have cured cancer. In 1772 Blicke published *An Essay on the Bilou or Yellow Fever of Jamaica* in which he mentions that – along with bleeding, purging, warm baths, fresh and acid drinks – water from the hot wells of Bristol should be sent to the West Indies as a curative.

Then there was Sir Hans Sloane (1660–1753), president of the Royal Society and founder of the British Museum. He sold a patent eye salve and advertised the beneficent effects of milk chocolate. He also wrote prescriptions containing centipedes and millipedes. One of his favourite cure-alls was viper's both. Here is the recipe:

> Take one living viper and remove the head, tail and viscera, excepting the heart and liver. Cut into little pieces and mix it with blood and add well-water twelve ounces. Put in a closed vessel, boil for two hours and strain, and the broth will be made.

For legal reasons, readers of this book must be warned not to try any of the curious cures mentioned here at home. Even the ones that do not kill you or leave you debilitated for life are likely to be very unpleasant – particularly the viper's both. Read them purely for entertainment. Remember that people in old England tried these radical and often revolting remedies because they were desperate back when, as Hobbes said, life was nasty, brutish and short. Just count your blessings that we live in a time when there are anaesthetics, antiseptics, painkillers, modern drugs, laboratories, regulatory authorities, teaching hospitals, well-trained doctors, skilled surgeons, autoclaves, drips, transfusions, transplants, monitors and the whole panoply of modern scientific medical equipment.

CHAPTER ONE

Bleeding Cures

T SEEMS SHOCKING to us in the days of blood transfusions that doctors in old England thought that the cure for almost any condition – including blood loss – was to open a vein and let the gore flow forth. Bloodletting had been used as a therapy since ancient Egyptian times and the father of medicine, Hippocrates, who lived in Greece in the fifth and fourth centuries BC, recommended it.

Hippocrates developed a theory about why bleeding was good for you. He reckoned that health was regulated by the four humours – yellow bile, black bile, blood and phlegm. A person became ill when these humours got out of balance, hence the need for bleedings, purges, vomitings, sweatings and blisterings.

Blood, of course, was the most vital of the humours. It carried the spirit of the body. In ancient Rome, the blood of freshly slain gladiators was drunk as a tonic, and drinking blood was long thought to be the cure for consumption, as tuberculosis used to be known. However, this remedy could have dire consequences. In the eighteenth century, a physician reported that an epileptic girl who drank the blood of a cat to cure herself developed feline characteristics and went about screeching and climbing on roofs.

Taking sides

In the sixteenth century a debate raged over whether you should draw blood from the same side as the ailment, or the opposite side. This only ended with the discovery of the circulation of blood by William Harvey in 1616. Until then it had been assumed that blood ebbed and flowed like the tide.

The implication of Harvey's discovery took some time to sink in. The famous English herbalist Nicholas Culpeper (1616–54) believed that a 'hot' liver, which produced sweet spittle and red urine, could be cured by bleeding the right arm. Followers of Ambroise Paré (1510–90) opened that same arm to stop bleeding from the left nostril. The veins of the feverish were opened to let the blood cool and women's ankles were cut to bring on menstruation.

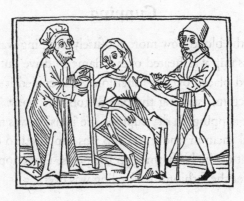

How much?

The problem with bleeding was that no one was sure how much blood you should take. One eleventh-century doctor believed that you could safely drain four-fifths of a human's blood. Generally, physicians continued to bleed a patient until they reached a point called 'syncope', when the patient would lose all sensation and faint, and the heartbeat would be weak. Today doctors would call that 'shock'.

Despite Harvey's discovery, bleeding was still widely used at the end of the eighteenth century. Rebellious old English colonist George Washington died the day after going out horseback riding in the snow. He was suffering from quinsy, or acute laryngitis which was treated with gargles of molasses, vinegar and butter, and a blister of cantharides – a preparation of dried beetles – which was placed against his throat. Meanwhile he was bled heavily four times, losing nine pints of blood in twenty-four hours. Not surprisingly, he died, aged 59 on 12 December 1799. It is not recorded whether his doctor was British.

Cupping

To make the blood flow more profusely, cupping was used. A small glass cup was heated over a flame to drive out some of the air and placed over the incision. As it cooled it created a partial vacuum, sucking the blood from the body. This was called wet cupping. In dry cupping, no incision was made and the partial vacuum under the cup was supposed to draw the disease out of the body through the pores. Dry cupping continued after the fashion for bleeding was over.

In the eighteenth century, cups were fitted with syringes to draw the air out. In the nineteenth century, rubber cups were used, as they were less fragile and easier to manipulate. In 1883 a device known as Juno's Boot was patented. This was clamped around an entire limb, sealed and, by means of a pump and valve, a vacuum was created so that the whole of an arm or leg could be cupped at one time.

Scarification

If one cut is good, more must be better. In scarification a series of small cuts was made in the skin to the depth of around an eighth of an inch.

Until the beginning of the sixteenth century, the cuts were made with a normal knife or scalpel. Then elaborate scarificators were made. They had between 12 and 20 spring-loaded blades which, when triggered, would cut a parallel grille of incisions. In 1813 a device was made that cut in different directions to produce a pretty latticework pattern. Scarificators were made in silver and ivory. They often came with a set of finely blown glass cups in a presentation set – the perfect gift for a medical man.

Blistering

Blistering was also used to divert the blood flow in the body in a number of inflammatory conditions. This was done by applying a mustard plaster or wax or resin mixed with cantharides – usually, Russian or Spanish flies. The irritation this causes first dilates the capillaries, drawing the blood to the skin. The blood plasma seeps out to form blisters, which can then be burst. This extremely unpleasant practice was ended when it was discovered that prolonged exposure to the cantharides damaged the kidneys.

Leech craft

Leeches were used as a method of bleeding. In the fourteenth century they were used to cure skin diseases; in the sixteenth for restoring menstruation. They were favoured over other methods of cutting when bleeding was required in sensitive areas such as around the eyes, in the mouth or on the sexual organs. Young brides also found them a useful cure for a prematurely misplaced maidenhead. On the wedding night, a leech was slipped into the vagina. When the eager groom entered the bride, he would dislodge the leech, producing a convincing deluge of blood, and everyone would be happy.

In normal use, the leech's tail would be cut off so that it could continue sucking for a long time without getting full. The blood would be sucked in one end and dribble out of the other. Leeches would be applied all over for general bleeding purposes, or on the ear to cure earache or the throat for tonsillitis. Gout, whooping cough, tumours and even mental illness were all treated by the application of leeches. When used to treat inflammation of the anus, a thread would be tied to the leech's tail to prevent it from disappearing all the way up the orifice. Varieties from Germany and Sweden were favoured as they were thought to be particularly voracious.

As leeches have a limited lifespan, artificial ones were made at the height of the leech craze between 1825 and 1840. The most famous was Heurteloup's Artificial Leech. This punctured a hole in the skin in the shape of a leech bite and had a large syringe barrel to suck the blood out. However, the real ones were better as they provided their own anticoagulant and tended to be gentler than any artificial device.

The use of the medical leech *Hirudo medicinalis* fell out of fashion at the end of the nineteenth century, but in the 1960s they began to be used again when tissue was being grafted or severed body parts were being reattached. Leech saliva helps re-establish blood flow. It contains not just an anticoagulant, but also vasodilators that widen the blood vessels, an anaesthetic and a natural antibiotic. Leeches prevent blood clots from forming and blood from forming pools within the tissue.

Blood in the stars

Medical calendars, almanacs, tables and wheel charts for bloodletting were published in the Middle Ages. They depicted the signs of the zodiac, which related the bleeding of different parts of the body to different conjunctions of the planets. However, the thirteenth-century English philosopher Roger Bacon had a simple rule. He said that bloodletting 'should be performed on a Saturday... on account of the malignity of Saturn who generates ill-fortune in all things'.

At the end of the fourteenth century, physicians were legally required to calculate the position of the moon before embarking on an operation. As late as the seventeenth century, many doctors doubled as astrologers and drew up individual charts that allied the parts of the body to certain star signs. The stars were thought to influence the strength and effectiveness of certain medicines and medical procedures. For example, a patient should not be bled when the moon was in the same sign as the body part being drained.

All this was swept away by the Age of Reason. In the eighteenth century, people were bled regularly in the spring and autumn to ensure they were in peak condition to face the summer and winter.

Bloodthirsty pirates

Thomas Dover was well known in the eighteenth century as the 'quicksilver doctor', for his liberal use of mercury as a cure-all. He was also the progenitor of Dover's Powder, which older readers might remember. Before he went into practice as a physician, Dover was a pirate, and in 1708 he commanded a privateer that sacked Guayaquil in Peru.

Pirate ships were overcrowded and unhealthy, so the young Dover had plenty of opportunity to hone his talents. During an epidemic on board, he bled 108 sailors. He took 100 ounces of blood from each of them. That's nearly three litres, half the capacity of the human circulatory system. Few of them would have been up to much yo-ho-hoing after that. On the same voyage, incidentally, Dover rescued Alexander Selkirk from the Juan Fernandez Islands. Selkirk's memoir of being marooned there provided the inspiration for Daniel Defoe's *Robinson Crusoe*.

Bloodless Mary

Mary, Queen of Scots suffered from stomach ulcers through-out her life, particularly at times of stress. In 1566, when she was visiting her lover, the Earl of Bothwell, in Jedburgh and planning the murder of her husband, she vomited so much blood that it was feared her life was in danger. A certain Dr Arnault was called. Fortunately he did not hold with bleeding, which was nearing the height of its fashion. If he had favoured it, she would almost certainly have died. Instead he did the opposite. He tied off her limbs with bandages. This minimised the peripheral blood flow, increasing the flow to her heart and brain. He also increased her intake of fluid by getting her to drink wine.

After a month, Mary was well enough to travel back to Edinburgh, where her troublesome spouse was disposed of. But this was not the end of stress for Mary, as she had hoped. She was deposed and imprisoned. Later, after her supporters had been routed, she fled to England where, after 18 years of captivity, her ulcers were finally cured by radical surgery: she was brutally bled by an English axe man.

CHAPTER TWO

Vomits and Purges

 N OLD ENGLAND, powerful laxatives to purge the bowels and emetics to induce vomiting were used as cures for headaches, fever, bowel disorders, venereal disease, deafness and insanity. Such practices had a long provenance. The ancient Egyptians believed that regular defecation was so important to good health that they had specialists called 'Shepherds of the Anus'. The pharaoh had his own personal rectal herdsman. The Greek writer Herodotus noted in the fifth century BC that 'the Egyptians use laxatives three days in a row and care for their health through vomit inducers and enemas, because they are of the opinion that all human illness originates from meals they enjoyed'. The English were of much the same opinion, which explains why the cuisine of old England was so bad.

Clearing the way

When treating a patient with any medicine, doctors in the eighteenth century commonly thought it sensible to paint on a fresh canvas, so they cleared out the system before they began. Purges and clysters, or enemas, were used to flush things downwards, while vomits and emetics brought them up. Doctors would examine the stool and bile closely before prescribing.

Don't vomit

A medicine salesman named Tom Jones condemned doctors who 'prescribed one sort of physick for all distempers, that is a vomit'. He satirised them in these words:

> If a man bruises his elbow, take a vomit, says the doctor. If you have corns: take a vomit. If he has torn his coat: take a vomit. For the jaundice, fevers, flux, gripes, gout, stone and pox, nay even those distempers known only to my friend the famous Dr Tufts, whom you all know, as the hockogrocles, marthambles, the moon-pall and the strong-fives: take a vomit.

Tufts was a well-known quack who lived in the Three Compasses in Maiden Lane. It is amazing how many seventeenth- and eighteenth-century doctors seemed to live and practise in pubs. When Tufts arrived in London, he revealed that 'after 40 years study, he hath discovered several strange diseases, for which (though as yet not known to the world) he had infallible cures'. 'Now the names of these new distempers are,' he said in a handbill:

THE STRONG FIVES, THE MOON PALL, THE MAR-THAMBLES AND THE HOCKOGROCLE. Although the names, natures, symptoms and several cures of these new diseases are altogether unknown to our greatest physicians and the particular knowledge of them would (if conceal'd) be a vast advantage to the aforesaid person; yet he, well knowing that his country's good is to be prefer'd to his private interest, doth hereby promise all sorts of people, a faithful cure of all any of the diseases aforesaid, at reasonable rates as our modern doctors have for that of any common distemper.

However, dear reader, if you find yourself coming down with the hockogrocles, marthambles, the moon-pall or the strong-fives, don't bother consulting your GP or going to hospital. They won't be able to do anything for you, as your condition will be a mystery to modern medical science.

Jones dismissed Tufts and other vomit-prescribing doctors as 'tag-rag-assifetide-glister-pipe-doctors', and then presented his own range of wares.

'Now gentlemen, having given you a short account of this spurious race,' he said:

I shall present you with my Cordial Pills, being the Tincture of the Sun. They cause all complexions to laugh or smile in the very taking of them, and cure all dizziness, dullness in the head and scurvy. My Incomparable Balsam heals all sores, curt and ulcers, old and new. The next I present you with is my Specifick, which certainly cures all agues in minutes. The last and most useful medicine prepared throughout the world is my Pulvis Catharticus. Its virtues are such, it will, equally with unicorn's horn, expel the rankest poison, 'tis a perfect and speedy cure and fortifies the heart against all faintness.

Powdered unicorn horn was the ultimate cure-all in the seventeenth century. Elizabeth I, it was said, bought a unicorn horn that reputedly cost her £10,000. That's £1.2 million in today's money.

The Perpetual Pill

Most patent medicines such as those Jones was selling were made out of powerful laxatives. In the eighteenth century, antimony was used. Not only would this send you rushing to the bathroom, but it would also deliver you prematurely to the grave. Antimony has much the same effect on the body as arsenic.

Even so, some bright spark came up with the 'Perpetual Pill'. It was a solid pellet of antimony. Once swallowed, it would pass right through the system. Recovered at the other end, it was washed off and used again.

Thankfully, the founder of Methodism John Wesley had a gentler remedy. As well as being an evangelist, he fancied himself as an amateur physician. While brother Charles was writing inspiring hymns, John wrote his medical bible, the *Primitive Physic*, first published in 1747. In it he recommended holding a puppy against the stomach as a cure for constipation.

The king of the purgers

It is certainly not a good idea to take a medicine that is going to kill you and plainly a doctor who makes up diseases with unknown symptoms can be dismissed as a quack. But surely a man who has healed himself can be trusted? One such was James Morison. His complaint? 'Total want of sleep, constant beating and uneasiness about the heart, dejection, the feeling of something like a bar about the lower part of my breast, no relish for amusement, nor anything else, and costiveness' – that is, constipation.

His condition was nothing if not persistent. 'Thirty-five years of inexpressible suffering is an event which falls to the lot of a few, if any at all,' he said. During those years, he 'ran the gauntlet of all the remedies: change of air [he tried living in Germany, Bordeaux in France, the West Indies and on the Gulf of Riga in the Baltic], country amusements, anthelmintics [the expelling of parasitic worms from the intestine], mercurial and mineral purges, stomactics [medicines for diseases of the mouth] and bitters, port wine and beef steak, cold baths, chalybeates [water containing iron] and mineral water, mercury in all its shapes, salivation, valerian [a drug made from the root of heliotrope], ether, bark in abundance, laxative pills and diets'.

If that was not enough, 'the truss maker was set to work. Steel jackets were made to spread out the bones of my chest.' When this did not help, he went under the knife. On the advice of two physicians and two surgeons, he had his xiphisternum – the cartilaginous tip of the beast bone – removed. Afterwards Morison continued 'struggling with disease, the powers of energy of life fast subsiding, the faculties becoming impaired and the sight becoming dim'.

By this time Morison was 52. He decided that he had suffered long enough and began to study pharmacy. Soon he concluded that all his symptoms were caused by the 'bad humour' his 'stomach and bowels had diffused over his body'.

What he needed was violent purging, and he developed his 'Vegetable Universal Compound, to purify the blood and systems'. It was a powerful laxative made from aloes, jalap, gamboges, colocynth, cream of tartar, myrrh and rhubarb. It was so powerful that after 12 months use he passed a 'substance of a skinny, glutinous nature – four or five inches long, moulded like the gut, which descended from the mouth of the stomach, immediately below the place where the learned doctors and surgeons had begun their incision'.

Soon all of Morison's symptoms disappeared, he said. So he fashioned his Vegetable Universal Compound into pills and sold them, using an illustration of the mysterious object he had passed as part of his advertising. His pills were so successful that he decided his cure must reach a wider audience than he could cater for alone. In 1828 he set up the British College of

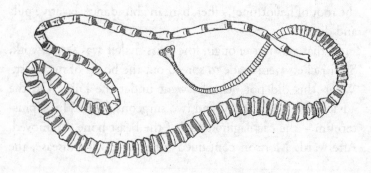

Health in Hamilton Place, King's Cross, London, where he trained other practitioners in the art of purging.

Morison's principle was clear and straighforward. 'It is impossible that there can be any real cure but by sound purging,' he said. If two or three of his pills did not produce the required results, try 12 or 13 before bedtime. It was not uncommon for a hygeist to recommend doses of 15 or 20 pills at the onset of an illness. In *Morisoniana*, a collection of his writings published after his death, Morison wrote: 'Patients have taken 30, 40 and 50 pills at a time in severe and urgent cases; and what was the consequence? Nothing but that they were sooner well.'

Others argued that overuse of the pills killed people. There were lawsuits. At one trial, a grocer swore on oath that he had taken 18,000 pills. The popularity of Morison's pills was scarcely dented when, in 1836, a hygeist was actually convicted of manslaughter after a man who had come to him with rheumatism of the knee died following a course of treatment. The post-mortem revealed that 'large and excessive quantities of pills' were the cause of death. Even so, agents were sent out across the Continent and the Empire, peddling pills. In New York state alone, $150,000-worth of Morison's pills were consumed.

Morison's pills were even a cure for syphilis. 'All persons acquainted with, and practising the use of Vegetable Universal Compound, will not have to dread the contagion of this disease,' he said. 'They will prevent and cure, if already caught.'

The 'flesh brush'

Purging played an important part in Morison's broader view of life as expressed in his papers *Some Important Advice to the World* and *A Treatise on the Origin of Life*, published by the British College of Health. Yet although Morison believed his purgative was a cure-all, even he knew there was one problem with it. It only worked internally. For the outside of the body what was required was a sound thrashing with a 'flesh brush'. 'This was the only external application the body requires,' said Morison, 'as the Vegetable Universal Medicine is the only internal one.'

This was very much in keeping with the times. In the late eighteenth and early nineteenth centuries, flagellation was very much in vogue. Fashionable ladies joined spanking clubs as a way to enjoy a sexual frisson without risking pregnancy or venereal disease.

Men flocked to celebrity whippers. Even George IV was reported to have visited Mrs Collett in Tavistock Court. The most famous of these thrashers was Mrs Teresa Berkeley, who kept her famed 'Berkeley Horse' at 28 Charlotte Street. This was a padded trestle where gentlemen callers or 'anyone with plenty of money could be birched, whipped, fustigated [cudgelled], scourged, needle-pricked, holly-brushed, furze-brushed [tormented with gorse], or phlebotomised [made to bleed], until he had had a bellyful'. It was, of course, therapeutic. Even John Wesley said that a good going over with a flesh brush brought roses to your cheeks.

Morison was persuaded of the efficacy of the flesh brush by Admiral Henry of Rolvenden in Kent, who had become 'very infirm from rheumatism and other disorders, and accordingly he began beating and hammering all the parts affected with hard instruments made for the purpose'. This, apparently, cured him.

As if, with all those purges, Morison had not suffered enough, he soon found that the flesh brush 'passed with a strong hand over every part of the body for a good while twice a day... prepares you for exercise and prevents fatigue'. It 'loosens and detaches gummy humours under the skin and parts adjacent'. These are then carried off by the blood to the bowels, where they are removed by his vegetable cleansers. The problem was that Admiral Henry's instruments were 'all of a violent description, made out of bits of wood, but finding these excoriated the skin, bone was tried and answered the object in view'.

It seems to me that there are practical problems with being beaten while being fed powerful laxatives. Think of the mess. Nevertheless, titled patients wrote testimonials, saying how Morison's remedies had cured them, their husbands and their maids. A petition was even delivered to Parliament asking for a select committee to be set up to evaluate the hygeian system in the interest of medical science.

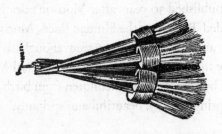

Later developments

It is said that Morison was reaching for his pills when he died at the age of 70 in 1840. He left £500,000 – £30 million at today's prices – and was laid to rest in a huge family tomb in Kensal Green Cemetery. His portrait was hung in the National Portrait Gallery. There was a proposal to raise a monument to Morison in front of the British College of Health. Contributions were to be limited to one penny from all those who had benefited from taking his pills. In response, the weekly humorous magazine *Punch* suggested that a slab of monumental brass be laid in the English churchyard fullest of the patients Morison's pills had killed.

The British College of Health long outlived Morison. In 1859 it published an enquiry into Morison's hygeian system. This continued to extol the virtues of purgation, which was 'destined to live and prosper, when allopathy [the curing of one disease by inducing another], homoeopathy, mesmerism and all other baseless systems shall have ceased to perplex and deceive suffering humanity'. By 1868 the seven principles of hygeism Morison had expounded in 1835 and been extended to 18.

Morisoniana sold over 110,000 copies at a shilling (5p) each when it was published 30 years after Morison's death. In it, in a section headed 'Perfecting the Human Race', Morison wrote: 'The hygeist and his agents have seen enough to convince them that, by their use of the Vegetable Universal Medicines, administered by parents to their children from birth, they will see their offspring healthy, beautiful and sprightly.'

CHAPTER THREE

Odd Ailments

N OLD ENGLAND THERE were a number of odd
ailments that no one seems to suffer from today
– and these are not just the hockogrocles, mar-
thambles, the moon-pall or the strong-fives that
Dr Tufts made up.

Greensickness

Up until the nineteenth century, the disease chlorosis, or
greensickness, was common among young women. It caused
them to swoon at the slightest suggestion of impropriety
and their pale skin turned a greenish yellow. This was because
their blood lacked iron as a result of a poor diet and a lack of
fresh air. These days, thanks to improvements in living conditions, women rarely swoon and chlorosis is confined to plants,
where it is a disease that stops the chlorophyll in the leaves
developing.

The king's evil

For centuries scrofula – a tuberculous swelling of the lymph glands – was also known as 'the king's evil'. This was because it could be cured by the touch of a monarch.

Edward the Confessor, who is said to have cured 1,736 people just by touching them, first used the royal cure in England. Charles II is said to have touched more than 90,000 sufferers between 1660 and 1682. The renowned surgeon Richard Wiseman (1620–76) wrote: 'I myself have been a frequent eye-witness of many hundreds of cures performed by his majesty's touch alone, without any assistance of chirurgery; and those, many of them, such as had tired out the endeavours of able chirugeons before they came thither.'

Charles's nephew William of Orange tried to end the practice, which he regarded as superstition. Forced to touch one patient, he said dismissively: 'May God grant you better health and more sense.' However, his sister-in-law Queen Anne resumed the cure, but she was the last royal healer in England.

She touched 200 sufferers in 1712. One of them was the young Samuel Johnson, who was also given a 'touch piece' – a gold token that was thought to have curative properties of its own. Neither worked, as Dr Johnson underwent painful surgery to drain the lymph glands later in life. Queen Anne herself was one of eight English monarchs to suffer from gout. When she died of dropsy in 1714, she was so swollen with retained fluid that she had to be buried in a square coffin.

Cures for a monarch

When Charles II faced the final curtain, his doctors were unsure of their diagnosis, but not for want of trying. Charles seems to have been struck down by apoplexy or a stroke in 1658. Desperate to keep his brother and chosen successor James – who had already declared himself a Catholic – from the throne, Charles's doctors administered 58 different drugs to the dying king. They also ran through the whole gamut of cures – purges, vomits, cupping, bleeding and scarifying. He was given laxatives, bladder-easing plasters, emetics, sneezing powder, absinthe, ammonia, bitter-water, thistle leaves and at least two dozen other herbs. A potion of liquorice and sweet almond in decocted oats was used to relax him, while pigeon excrement was smeared on his feet. When that did not work, he was given 40 drops of extract from a man's skull. He spent his last five days on earth with hot irons on his feet.

None of it did any good. The autopsy showed that his body was so full of blood that he could not have survived. Dr Scarburgh, one of a dozen physicians who treated the dying king, said, not without some satisfaction, 'Nothing was left untried.'

'The leaf'

A caul is the inner membrane enclosing the foetus before birth that sometimes envelops the head of the child at birth. Once it was thought of as a good omen that would preserve the individual against drowning. However, in seventeenth-century London, there seems to have been an epidemic of such births with morbid complications. Fortunately, a physician came up with a cure called 'Electuarium Mirable' and decided to give a lecture about the condition and its remedy.

The lecture was advertised in a handbill that read:

All curious gentlemen, physicians and others, who shall think themselves concern'd, that on Thursday the 28th of this instant July, will be read at Stationer's Hall, a lecture of 'Anatomy on the Caul and its use in infants'; wherein it will be plainly proved, that that membrane in brutes vulgarly called the Leaf and by physicians the Caul, is generally consum'd or waste away in newly born children that die afterwards of gripes and convulsions, which proceed from this Tabes Omentalis or Consumption of the Caul; and further, it will hereby be manifested that the want of that part is the real cause that this disease becomes so universally mortal, and is now grown as it were epidemical in London.

The Author designs to satisfie the publick at once in the truth of this discovery by Evident Demonstration, and he has delivered out tickets at a guinea [around £100 today] each, to be had at White's Chocolate-House and the Smyrna Coffee-house near St James', Tom's Coffee-house in Covent Garden and Batson's Coffee-house in Corn-hill.

The handbill concludes by announcing that the 'Electuarium Mirable' can be obtained from the Golden Ball in Princess Street, near Stocks Market.

French scurvy

It was advantageous to a practitioner if he had not only a new cure, but also a new disease. A certain 'J.T.', who advertised himself as a

> …licensed physician… who liveth in the Upper Moorfields at the Globe and Two Balls, addresses himself in recommending his Pilula Imperialis vel Sospitalis [Imperial or Salutory Pills], whose vertues and excellent qualities do aloud proclaim to the world the great benefit they bring to mankind, they being the only antidote to the French scurvy.

When it came to the French scurvy, J.T. had the field to himself. Even so, he apparently found some patients who he cured of this curious condition. One can only suppose that the French scurvy was a cross between regular scurvy and the French pox.

CHAPTER FOUR

Rural Remedies

I N OLD ENGLAND THERE were outlandish cures
that seem to be little more than old wives' tales.
In the countryside, however, they were practised
for hundreds of years for various conditions until
modern scientific medicine took over. They may have worked
simply through the placebo effect, but they must have done
some good or they would have been abandoned.

Headaches

The book *Old-Fashioned Remedies* recommended placing a
cabbage leaf or large lettuce leaf in your hat to keep your head
cool and prevent headaches caused by the heat. The Tudors
purged their heads by 'gargarisms' – gargling. Mustard was
used. A spoonful of mustard in the mouth was also a cure for
lethargy. And the Tudor cure for 'rheum in the head' was to
boil pimpernel in wine and drink it cold in the morning and
hot in the evening.

One sure cure for a headache was to tie a piece of hangman's rope around your skull. These were readily available in the eighteenth century because of the number of public hangings. Hangmen made a healthy living selling off ropes fresh from the gallows, which they had cut up into short pieces.

In the nineteenth century, snakeskin was substituted. Otherwise you could rub your temples with half an onion or apply a poultice made of raw potato. There was also opium.

Foot and mouth

Old-Fashioned Remedies says that urine is good for anything to do with the feet. It recommends: 'When they are sweaty and aching or if you have got athlete's foot, blisters or bruises, soak your feet in a bowl of hot urine.' Fresh urine was also recommended as a mouthwash.

Medicine cupboard

Old Corner Cupboard prescribes liquid paraffin for opening the bowels, while two drops of turpentine on a lump of sugar cured chesty coughs. Dung from a fresh cowpat was used to 'draw' a boil – although you could, of course, drink your own urine or a glass of warm water with gunpowder in it.

Earache

There is a wide selection of things you can stick in your ear if you have problems in that quarter: black wool, a clove of garlic dipped in honey, a cockroach dipped in oil, snail juice – a cure for almost every malady – and ant eggs beaten in onion juice. The *Primitive Physic* says that, for earache caused by the cold, you should boil rue, rosemary or garlic and direct the steam into the ear with a funnel.

Warts

For warts, John Wesley said: 'Rub warts daily with any one of the following: a radish, juice of dandelion or marigold flowers, mole's blood or swine's blood, fasting spittle, elder leaves or flowers and finally eat largely of watercress.' *The Bedale Book of Witchcraft* of 1773 recommends: 'Frog spit rubbed on a wart or rubbed on a pig's back, or wash your hand with water in which eggs have been boiled are certain cures.'

The monks of Glastonbury had a more decorous treatment. When an epidemic of 'warty eruptions' swept through the Abbey in the tenth century, they cured them by having a virgin hang seven wafers around their necks.

Otherwise you could rub a piece of stolen beef on a wart, after which it was thrown in the midden; throw pieces of knotted string, one for each wart, in the privy; rub warts with snails, impale the snails on thorns and watch them dry out, or tie horse's hair around a wart and watch it drop off.

Coughs and sneezes

For the common cold, you could try soaking a thick piece of toast in vinegar and binding it to your throat with a handkerchief. Otherwise you must go to bed at night with a filthy sock or stocking around your neck with the heel over your larynx. Alternatively, you could try sticking orange peel up your nostrils.

Chest complaints were to be warded off by strapping rashers of bacon to the ribcage, or you could try a vest made of brown papers and goose fat, with extra grease on the feet. If you came down with bronchitis, the old English remedy was to go out into the fields in the early morning and lie down on one of the warm patches of grass where a cow had slept. Otherwise, you could try inhaling the breath of a cow.

Tumours

A fifth-century cure for a tumour involved cutting a root in half. One half was hung around the patient's neck. The other half was thrown on a fire and, as it shrivelled, so would the tumour. If the patient did not then pay up, the doctor would take the shrivelled root from the fire and drop it in water. As the root reconstituted and grew back into shape, so would the tumour. Alternatively, you could try burning the brains of a mad dog and applying the ashes.

Whooping cough

According to the Thackray Medical Museum in Leeds, the old Yorkshire cure for a child with whooping cough was to pass it under the belly of a donkey. This was particularly popular in Scarborough, where there were numerous donkeys for hire. However, John Wesley's *Primitive Physic* says: 'For the chin-cough or whooping cough, rub the feet thoroughly with hog's lard before the fire, at going to bed, and keep the child warm. Swallow four wood lice alive in a spoonful of jam or treacle and the "whoop" will vanish.'

The Bedale Book of Witchcraft says: 'A field mouse skinned and made into a small pie then eaten, the warm skin bound hair-side to the throat, and kept there for nine days will cure the worst whooping cough.' Also: 'Catch a frog, open its mouth then cough into it three times, then throw the frog over your left shoulder for luck.'

In seventeenth-century Ireland, a live trout would be placed to the mouth of a child with whooping cough. It was then thrown back into the water and would carry off the disease.

For those who could not run to a trout, again a frog would do. If there were no frogs around, you could take a mug of water, filled against the stream. A mouthful would be given to the child to drink and the rest thrown back. This was to be done just before daybreak, three mornings running.

Or else you could pluck a hair from the head of the sufferer and feed it to a dog. When it stuck in the animal's throat and it tried to cough it up, it was thought that the disease had been transferred to the dog. In seventeenth-century Lincolnshire, children with whooping cough were fed fried mice.

In Norfolk the cure was tying up a spider in a muslin bag and hanging it over the mantelpiece. In Suffolk children had their heads pushed down a hole freshly dug in a meadow. In Yorkshire a broth made from owls was fed to an infected child, while in the West Country sufferers were fed cakes made from barley and child's urine.

In Scotland a sufferer was supposed to follow the instructions of any man who passed by on a piebald horse, while south of the border it was widely believed that riding a bear would do the trick. Martha Lloyd, Jane Austen's sister-in-law, recommended:

> Cut off the hair from the top of the head as large as a crown piece. Take a piece of brown paper of the same size: dip it in rectified oyl of amber, and apply it to the part for nine mornings, dipping the paper fresh each morning. If the cough is not removed, try it again after three or four days.

Eye complaints

In Tudor times it was recommended 'for eyes that are blasted… only wear a piece of black sarcenet [fine, soft silk] before thy eyes, and meddle with no medicine; only forbear wine and strong drink', while in the sixth century, patients suffering from cataracts were urged to catch a fox, tear out its tongue, then release the animal back into the wild. The tongue should then be carried around wrapped in a red rag.

Otherwise sore eyes could be cured by binding the lungs of a hare over them. The rest of the hare should not go to waste. The brain stewed in wine was a sedative, while carrying the ankle staved off cramp. Licking the eyes of a frog was also recommended.

Other remedies thought to be effective for eye problems included the spittle of a starving peasant, dried human excrement, chicken's dung, a salve of lizard and bat's blood, blood drawn from the tail of a black cat and, in the eighteenth century, a large draft of beer drunk every morning.

Best of all, the thirteenth-century Anglo-Saxon manuscript *Leechdoms, Wortcunning and Starcraft of Early England* – which is the equivalent of *Conventional Medicine, Herbal Alternatives and Astrology* in modern English – recommends that a man take 'mead or woman's milk' as a cure for blindness. Three teaspoons full of woman's milk is recommended merely for 'dimness of the eyes'.

Rheumatism

One cure for rheumatism – and even paralysis – involved collecting 30 pennies in the church porch 'without asking for any'. They were then exchanged for a silver coin from the offertory by the priest. After that the sufferer would have to hobble around the communion table three times. The coin would then be taken to the blacksmith, who would fashion it into a ring. After three weeks of wearing the ring the patient was cured – unless, as was often the case, the blacksmith kept the silver and made the ring out of a cheaper metal.

Rings made from coffin nails or hinges cured cramp. Cramp could be prevented by hanging a rusty sword on the wall by the bed, or by putting a piece of brimstone or a potato under the mattress.

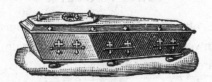

Calendar dates and cures

The calendar played its part in treatment. Cornish children suffering from rickets were always bathed on the first Wednesday in May. The Scots believed that any illness would be worst on a Sunday, while the English thought that Friday was a good day to take medicine – after all, the communion bread on a Good Friday, particularly, promised everlasting life.

In Anglo-Saxon times it was thought that the first day of March and four days before the end of that month were good times to start treatment. There were different combinations of days for each month. By the seventeenth century, the date an illness started fixed the prognosis: 'Number the days from 26 June, to the day when a party first began to fall sick, and divide by three. If one remain, he will long be sick; if two, he will die; if none, he will quickly recover.'

The sixth-century physician Aetius employed numerology in his cures. Consequently, his cure for gout changed with the month. 'In September,' he prescribed, 'milk only. October, eat garlic. November, no bathing. December, eat cabbage. January, wine every morning. February, no beets. March, sweets must be mixed with all food and drink. April, avoid horse-radish. May, no fish. June, cold water every morning. July, abstinence. August, no mallows.'

Tudor remedies

Tudor houses often had physic gardens where medicinal herbs such as wormwood, mandrake, valerian, plantain, pennyroyal, tansy and harefoot would be grown. The women of the house would make 'syrup of poppy' for toothache or to soothe a restless child, while the worms thought to cause tooth decay could be flushed out with boiled green frog, and hare's brain would be administered to an infant when teething.

When there was an outbreak of 'sweating sickness' in 1528, the recommended remedy was 'treacle and water imperial, which doth drive it from the heart and thus have helped them that have swooned divers times'. Other cures for the sweat were a mixture of mercury, marigold, endive and nightshade or, if you were rich enough, half a nutshell of unicorn's horn in three large spoonfuls of dragon's water.

Burnt feathers and dung were administered as a cure for quinsy or tonsillitis and to banish haemorrhoids:

> Take the sole of an old shoe worn by a man much used to travel; cut it into pieces, and burn it, yet neither to grey or white ashes, but to a friable tender coal. Reduce it into an impalpable powder. Take then unsalted hog lard, and work it to an ointment, and anoint the afflicted part often therewith.

Scurvy-grass

From the Middle Ages onwards, monks grew the herb known as spoonwort (*Cochlearia officinalis*) or, more commonly, scurvy-grass, in the physic gardens to make an infusion for sufferers of scurvy, which was particularly common in England in the seventeenth century. It also grew wild on sand dunes. John Gerard's *Herbal*, published in 1580, says: 'Our common scurvie grass groweth in divers places upon the brims of the River

Thames, as at Woolwich, Erith, Greenhithe and Gravesend, as well as on the Essex shore. The juice is given in ale or beere. It perfectly cures the disease called the Scurvie.'

A special ale with scurvy-grass added was prepared and dispensed by St Bartholomew's Hospital in 1669. The ale was supplied by a local brewer and in 1677 'the steward was empowered to buy four measures of pewter to be used in the scurvy-grass cellar', according to the journals of the hospital, 'but it was only to be given by the direction of the doctor'.

Compound Spirits of Scurvy-Grass

There were also proprietary brands of scurvy-grass. In 1664 a Mr Clark introduced his famous Compound Spirits of Scurvy-Grass. By 1694 he was relating a large number of cases where his cure had 'snatched people from death's door'. One of them was Mary Jones of Thetford, 'who had not been out of her house for the space of five years, but after taking two bottles, Mary went to church'.

Mr Clark's remarkable elixir did not stop short at curing scurvy. It also cured 'rheums, toothache, asthma and stones in the bladder'. However, it would not cure whatever Mr Clark had. 'For it hath pleased the Almighty to take to himself the said Mr Clark,' said a handbill advertising his Compound Spirits, 'yet the said Compound Spirits continue to be truly prepared by his widow at her dwelling house in Naked-Boy Court, near Strand Bridge, by the Maypole in the Strand, which are sealed with her coat of arms, the three swords in a fess [broad horizontal bar], price one shilling a bottle.'

Mrs Clark continued making the Clark's Compound Spirits of Scurvy-Grass for 16 years after her husband's death.

Essential Spirit of Scurvy-Grass

One Sieur de Vernantes claimed to the original inventor of 'Essential Spirit of Scurvy-Grass... communicated by him to Hen Clarke, chymist and apothecary of London and now by him prepared'.

He made even more extravagant claims for the medicine that he sold. 'This noble spirit, which from the hand of this great artist, I do offer to all who at this day suffer under the scurvey, and it also cures the dropsey even to a wonder.'

Golden Spirit of Scurvy-Grass

Thomas Blagrave made a Golden Spirit of Scurvy-Grass and found himself in a war of words with Robert Bateman, who claimed his Spirit of Scurvy-Grass was the 'true and only preparation'. Bateman also took on Sieur de Vernantes, whose product, he says, was 'lately shamm'd up on the world by one Clark, an ale-draper near Temple Barr'.

Bateman claimed that de Vernantes was once an apothecary's boy and was proficient at making vomits, but was now a 'drunkard maker' who laced his concoctions with strong liquor, serving up 'nappy bub or Compound Scurvey-Drinks at your pleasure'.

True Spirit of Scurvy-Grass

When Bateman died, his Spirit of Scurvy-Grass continued to be made by one Robert Smith. He found himself in competition with Dr Pordage of Leather Lane near Holbourn, who sold 'True Spirit of Scurvy-Grass' at sixpence a bottle and had a new method of distribution. According to his handbill:

> But the new ingenious way of the PENNY POST, any person may send for it from any part of the city or suburbs, writing plain directions where to send it.... But who sends this way must put a penny in the letter (besides sixpence for each glass) to pay the carriage back, for nobody can think the profit great; therefor a penny must be sent for every parcel. None need fear their money in sending by the PENNY POST, for things of considerable value are daily with safety sent by it, security being given by the messengers. There are houses appointed in all parts of the town to take the PENNY POST LETTERS.

The real cure

In fact, the Tudor sailor and adventurer Sir John Hawkins had discovered a more effective cure for scurvy long before. He dosed his entire ship's company with lemon juice. Lime juice was widely used in the eighteenth century, when Sir George Blane suggested the Royal Navy take it up. In 1795 the Navy made the use of lime as a cure for scurvy on board ships compulsory.

Cures for wounds

The sixteenth-century Swiss physician Paracelsus introduced chemistry to medicine and his cures circulated widely among the medical profession in old England. However, some of the treatments he recommended were bizarre.

To treat wounds, he recommended mixing red wine and earthworms with the 'moss' from the skull of a man recently killed or hanged, gathered when Venus was in the ascendant. Other medieval doctors favoured blood or human fat over skull moss. Fortunately, this deadly ointment was not applied to the wound itself, which was left covered by a piece of linen. The mixture was to be applied to the weapon that had caused the wound while it was still bloody. If that could not be found, a stick poked in the wound could be substituted. The treatment would have to be repeated four or five times until the wound healed.

By treating the instrument that caused injury, the wound itself healed 'sympathetically'. It worked. When shards of a bomb recovered from the head of Captain de Barke, who was injured at the siege of Stettin in 1676, were treated this way, he miraculously recovered and returned to the army.

Other sixteenth-century doctors said that wounds should be treated directly with *oleum catellorum* – live cats boiled in olive oil, though some preferred the more traditional folk remedy of covering wounds with spider's webs.

To get bones to knit, one Victorian medical almanac recommended ingesting powdered dog's skull, although generally folk medicine favours the more palatable drinking of comfrey tea.

In medieval times they went to great lengths to prevent wounds healing up too fast. Wounds would be opened with forceps or enlarged by cutting the flesh, then plugged until they suppurated, producing the pus thought to be vital to healing. In the sixteenth century, sticks were even forced between the broken ends of bones. The excruciating pain produced was thought to be part of the healing process.

A minor wound should be washed with a stone that had been heated and dropped into a pail of water. Other recommendations were treating cuts and abrasions with toasted cheese, mouldy bread, tobacco or calf's dung with crushed earthworms in it.

Diagnosing death

Even today it is difficult to know whether someone is dead or not. Medical science used to consider that you were dead if your heart stopped. Then in 1967, South African surgeon Christiaan Barnard performed a heart transplant and blew that theory right out of the water. It was then decided that you were dead if there was no detectable electrical activity in the brain. Even this is now under assault. There have been a number of cases where relatives have challenged medical opinion and gone to court, where a judge has been asked to decide whether someone on a life-support system who is in a persistent vegetative state is legally dead or not.

In old England things were even more problematic. It was

impossible to tell whether the patient was dead until putrefaction had set in. This presented the loved one's family with a dilemma. Everyone was terrified of premature burial. On the other hand, you did not want a corpse hanging around the home until it began to rot. So doctors came up with numerous tests. Salt and pepper were blown up the nose to see if the corpse would sneeze. Pieces of onion, garlic and horseradish were shoved up the nostrils in the hope that the acrid odour would revive the patient. Tobacco smoke blown up the anus was thought to revive the drowned, and one doctor even invented a machine to do this. Astringent enemas were administered. Trumpets were sounded in the ears. Vinegar, salt or warm urine was poured into the mouth. The body was whipped with stinging nettles. Hot wax was dripped on the scalp and the soles of the feet were slashed. Most extreme of all, a red-hot poker was applied to the anus just to see if the corpse would flinch.

CHAPTER FIVE

Universal Elixirs

S LONDON GREW TO become the biggest city in Europe, and then the world, it was filled with dirt and disease. It was, however, also a place full of optimism. People attracted to the city felt that they could become rich and move up the social ladder. Perhaps they would marry well, or attract the attention of the monarch and be given a title. If life could be so easily transformed, wasn't it at least possible that a wonderful new medicine could mend an ailing body? Wasn't it at least possible that some universal elixir could cure all ills? Wasn't it possible that some magical substance could banish disease altogether and give those who took it everlasting life?

Gold

In the sixteenth century, there was a great belief in the healing properties of gold. As it did not rust or decay, it seemed to embody the principles of immortality. Towards the end of the century, a young Englishman named Francis Anthony tried to harness its powers.

After graduating with a Master of Arts degree from Cambridge, Francis Anthony went to Hamburg to study medicine. Returning to London with a diploma, he began to practise. Soon he was hauled before the president and censors of the College of Physicians for practising without a licence. During cross-examination, Anthony admitted that he had 'practised physick in London for six months and during that period he had cured 20 or more divers diseases in people to whom he had given purging and vomiting physick. To others he had given a disphoretick [sweat-inducing] medicine prepared from gold and mercury.' He had no licence, and was fined £20 and jailed.

Released in 1602, he resumed his practice until fresh charges were laid against him 'by a Reverend Divine, who upon his deathbed, complained that a medicine called Aurum Potabile given him by Anthony had killed him'. Aurum Potabile is drinkable gold.

Speaking in his own defence in 1610, Anthony was forced to reveal the recipe for his elixir, although he kept the process for making it secret. It was, however, published in 1683 in

London by one William Cooper in a pamphlet called: 'Receit showing the way to make his most Excellent Medicine called AURUM POTABILE'.

First a block of tin was to be placed in an iron pan and heated until it turned into a powder the consistency of ashes. Four ounces of this powder was to be mixed with three pints of strong red wine and left to 'digest' for two or three days. The clear liquid produced was to be distilled, then added to a quart of red wine with another four ounces of the tin powder in it and left to digest for ten days. The result was to be filtered and distilled, and the residue mixed into a pint of vinegar. This was to be heated for ten days, and then distilled. The resulting distillate Cooper called the 'menstruum' – which means a liquid that dissolves a solid or holds it in suspension. Cooper continued:

> Then take one ounce of pure refined gold which costs £3 13s 4d, and file it into dust, heat it with an equal quantity of white salt and subject it to heat for four hours. Grind this very small and after calcining it [heating it to a high temperature without effecting a chemical or physical change], wash it with boiling water repeatedly. One ounce of the residue is to be then digested with half a pint of the menstruum and heated for six days. After again being distilled, the residuum dried and powdered, is to be put into half a pint of spirit of wine, left for ten days and then poured off.

This process is to be repeated three times, and then the liquors are to be distilled until they have the viscosity of syrup. 'One ounce of this is to be put into a pint of canary-sack [a wine from the Canary Islands] and the solution is ready for use.'

Despite the death of the clergyman, there was such a demand for this remedy that Anthony's son continued selling it after his father's death.

Golden ointment

The use of gold to cure all ills had a long provenance in old England. A Roman medical stamp found in Bath shows that a doctor named Junianus sold a 'golden ointment to clear the sight' to the citizens of Aquae Sulis, the city that the Romans had founded there.

Golden Elixir

The diet in seventeenth-century England was so poor that many people suffered from vitamin C deficiency. Fortunately the Golden Elixir – also known as the 'Herculeon Antidote' – was on sale, which could cure that 'popular disease, the scurvy'. The handbill advertising it went on to explain the many miraculous cures it had afforded:

Mr Davies on Thangue's Yard was cured of the bloody flux [dysentery] who had three impostumes [abcesses] as bit as a hen's maw, which was breeding 15 years, and was judged to be ptisick [suffering from pulmonary consumption]. Mr Yangley's daughter, who had worn away to an anatomy. Mrs French in Crown Court in Grub Street was quite distracted, occasioned by melancholick passion and was judged never to obtain her senses again, with this Elixir was cured. Mrs Price, a strong-waterman's wife at Wapping New Stairs, who was distracted and tore and broke all that she came near, now perfectly cured. Mrs Cock in Irish Court in Whitechapel, a Latin schoolmaster's wife, who was swelled as big as a barrel, and voided above 60 stones and had made use of several physicians, is now perfectly cured. Mrs Warren in Soaper's Alley, in Whitecross Street, being poysoned by eating mussels and swelled from head to foot, perfectly cured. Then there was Mr Field, the sexton of the Dutch church in Kattern-wheel Alley in Whitechappel, was worn to an anatomy and judged passed recovery, is now in perfect health. Also Mrs Fisher of Plasto, at the sign of the Green Man, of the wind cholick and lamesness, and Mr Febs at the Hand and Bowl in Barking, of a ptisical cough and mixt distempers all cured and well.

In other words, it could cure just about anything.

Elixir of youth

Even more remarkable was the 'Elixir Renovans' a physician in seventeenth-century London named Moses Stringer had developed. He claimed it was a cure for old age and, like any modern drug company, he had first tried it out on animals. He wrote a letter to the learned Dr Woodrofe, Master of Worcester College, Oxford, referring to himself in the third person, like most doctors of his time, saying:

That Learned Chymist made his first experiment up a hen, so very old, that nobody would kill it, either out of a sense of profit or good-nature. He mingled some of his medicine, which he called Renovating Quintessence, with a quantity of barley and gave it to the hen, 15 days together. The effects were wonderful, and the hen recovered youth and new feathers, and what is more surprising, LAID EGGS and hatcht chickens as if she had lost a dozen years of her age.

Following modern practice, he moved on to clinical trials:

An ancient woman that kept his house, with the consequences of old age, was on the very margin of death. He gave her the same medicine, 15 days together, as he had prescribed to his feathered patient and the success was the same. She recover'd her health, youth, hair and teeth again. Her complexion lookt florid and vigorous, and nature exerted itself as it generally does in young women.

Reflecting on these cures… I hope I have found a medicine which very much lessens the infirmities of age, renders nature vigorous and stretches the space of human life as far as Heaven permits.

Well, nobody could expect any more than that. Except for Dr Stringer who adds, emphatically, in capital letters: 'THE SAME MEDICINE CURES THE GOUT.'

In a second letter, Stringer extolled the virtues of his elixir and said that its effect on his patients was the 'it doth refresh them and make them young again'. But he warned, it was 'to be had only at my house, for fear of counterfeits, at a guinea a bottle, sealed with three eagles displayed'. And it was 'to be taken from fifteen drops to sixty at a time, four or five times a day in wine, ale, beer or water or in other proper infusion'.

By now he had tested it on his own family, he said. He 'first cured his mother, who was extremely swelled with the dropsie, having born 11 children, and was given over to the physicians'. Then he cured his 'wife's father who had his arm palsy-struck'.

There were other testimonials. 'Another remarkable case was the cure of one who had been a slave in Algiers in the year 1678, and by the ill-usage he had received, had a fever and calenture, scurvy, dropsie and palsy, one succeeding the other...' Calenture was a fever formerly supposed to affect sailors in the tropics. They would suffer from delirium, mistaking the sea for green fields and jumping in it. 'He was near 55, and continued a year in St Thomas's Hospital but could find no remedy. In this wretched condition he languished 20 years, until he took my "Renovating Elixir" and he is now absolutely recovered, and more plump and fat than ever he was in his life.'

Beams of light

If you could not afford an elixir made of gold, surely you should take a medicine which contained that equally incorruptible, though much more abundant substance – light. This was the claim of one Nathaniel Merry. 'His "Archael" or Vital Medicines are truly adapted for all times,' he said, 'being divested of their crudities and heterogene qualities, by a true separation of the pure from the impure, and impregnated with beams of light.'

Merry lived at 'The Star in Bow-lane, next but one to the Half-Moon Court for eight years'. Before the arrival of coffee houses, many of these doctors lived and practised in inns. He styled himself a 'philo-chym' and assured his patients: 'Such medicines I have always by me faithfully prepared by my own hands.'

His medicine could safely be taken in all weathers. 'There are many that perish in and around this city, through an evil custom arising from a false opinion, "That it is not safe to take physick in extreams of heat and cold or in the dog-days."'

Merry could apparently succeed where other physicians had failed. He claimed to have discovered the cure for the 'Dogmatical Incurables' and outlined his simple medical philosophy.

I have cured when the body hath been drawn double and fixt so, and the neck and face, drawn and fixt, looking over one shoulder, and have saved many hands, arms, legs, fingers and toes from cutting off, when they have been ready and order'd for amputation by the vulgar way. My cures have been

wrought by medicines, truly adapted and naturally gifted
with a capacity to expel and correct venoms and close with
nature centrally, by rays and beams of light upon the spirit
of life, which corrects the disorder of the Archaeus [the life
force according to the Paracelsus] and reunites its powers.

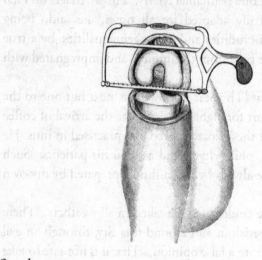

Sun beams

Another physician who sold light in an ingestible form was Dr
Lionel Lockyer. In 1680 he wrote a pamphlet extolling the
virtues of his *Pilulae Radiis Solis Extractae*. Everyone knows
that the sun's rays are good for you, so why not take them in
pill form?

He outlined 74 cases where he had prescribed these pills,
including one man who was 'cured of a regiment of diseases
and only by these pills'. Unfortunately, Lockyer admitted, other
diseases the poor chap had remained stubbornly incurable.

Then there was a patient 'who thought ill of the pills after taking one box'. Lockyer was dismissive. 'All such these many keep their money and their diseases too,' he said.

The good doctor, it seems, had an incurable condition too. After practising for at least 12 years, he died in 1672 and was buried in St Saviour's Church, Southwark. Plainly he had made a lot of money from his sunshine pills. His tomb boasts an effigy of the physician reclining on a pillow, wearing a large flowing wig and a fur-trimmed gown.

Mercury

If gold or sunbeams did not work there was always that universal cure-all, mercury. However, it is not without its side effects, as the renowned eighteenth-century Shakespearean actor Barton Booth discovered to his cost.

Booth was a legendary gourmand and by the time he was 40 his gluttony was getting the better of him. At the height of his career in 1727, he fell ill and was lost to the stage for six weeks. After that he suffered regular bouts of illness and developed severe jaundice. He thought that his career was over and could not believe his luck when he came across a book called *An Ancient Physician's Legacy to his Country*, published in 1732.

The physician who wrote the book was the previously mentioned former pirate Thomas Dover (see page 15). By then Dover had graduated as a Bachelor of Arts from Magdalen Hall, Oxford, and as a Bachelor of Medicine from Caius College, Cambridge. Known as the 'quicksilver doctor', he claimed that mercury was efficacious in 'leprosy, rheumatisms, the itch, inflammations and fluxions of the eyes, all cutaneous humours in the stomach and guts, stone, gravel and gout'.

There were already worries among some doctors, though, that mercury was poisonous. It had been noted that workers in mercury mines suffered from palsy and general debility. To be fair, it is the salts of mercury that are highly noxious. Mercury itself in relatively innocuous – unless you take large amounts of it.

When the cures Booth's own doctors prescribed for the repeated bouts of colic he suffered proved ineffective, he summoned Dover, who proposed a course of 'crude' mercury. Between 4 and 8 May 1733 Booth swallowed some two pounds of mercury and began to feel unwell. Nevertheless, he was still gulping the stuff down when his wife, the actress Hester Santlow, grew concerned and summoned another doctor. This was Sir Hans Sloane, who immediately had Booth bled. Nine fluid ounces of blood were drawn from his jugular vein and he was dosed with Sir Walter Raleigh's Cordial, a popular tonic of the day. It did no good. By 10 May Booth was sinking fast. He was experiencing excruciating headaches, so the doctor blistered his scalp. That evening he was dead.

The post-mortem found that the causes of Booth's problem

were gallstones that had blocked the bile duct and prevented bile discharging into the intestine. It was also found that the whole of Booth's digestive tract was full of mercury in globules the size of a pinhead. The intestines were 'as black as your hat' and 'would not endure the least straining without breaking to pieces'. Meanwhile the rectum was 'so rotten and blackened that it broke between my fingers like tinder'.

Although later that year Dover's methods were criticised by the surgeon Henry Bradley, this did not stop *An Ancient Physician's Legacy* going into numerous editions, bringing Dover fame, fortune and an international reputation.

Elixir for the Morow-Cure

Major John Choke styled himself 'the great traveller and one of His Majesty's chymists'. He sold an '*Elixir Capitalis totius Mundi* or the only Elixir in the World for the Morow-Cure of the gout, dropsie and agues of all sorts, tertian, quartan and quotidian.'

The recipe for Choke's Elixir came from his father-in-law, the famous Dutch physician and chemist Bapista van Helmot. Choke claimed it cured 'the Duke of Buckingham of an ague when all physicians had left him, and His Majesty was pleased to send for me, and as a mark of his Royal pleasure, give me his authority to practise in any of his dominions without any control'. His pupil Thomas Odored also cured a patient with the 'falling-sickness' who had been referred to him by the king.

The unfortunately named Odored also wrote a pamphlet dedicated to the Archbishop of Canterbury. Choke himself eschewed such things 'but for the good of such as have not much money to lay out upon physick, and such persons as can make appear that they are really poor, he will cure gratis. He lodgeth at the Blew Boar's Head and Chequer in the Strand, an Oyl hop, between St Clement's Church and the Maypole, near the Greyhound Tavern, where he may be spoken with every morning till ten or eleven a clock.'

A Noble Medicine

After 40 years as a 'citizen and surgeon of London' James Wasse decided to throw in the towel. 'Being himself now infirm by age, and not capable of doing his accustomed service to mankind,' he said, 'he is retiring to the country for his health, and therefore is resolved to publish the virtues, use and dose of his famous "Elixir".'

If Wasse was retiring to the country for his health, plainly the patient should do likewise. The Elixir has not healed its inventor. Nevertheless, Wasse's handbill went on: 'This Noble Medicine has, by the great industry and pains of the author, been brought to that perfection that no medicine hitherto made has answered the ends of this composition.'

Wasse's Elixir brought 'immediate ease to such as are troubled with gravel of any sort' – in the bladder and other internal organs – 'also as an antidote against all contagious diseases, either on ship-board or on shore, caused by corruption of the air, by bad provisions or any means whatsoever.'

Even though Wasse was retiring, the infirm did not need to despair. Nobly he was keeping his Elixir on sale. 'This Noble Medicine is to be had at the author's own house in Church-Alley in Celement's-lane, Lombard-street, also at several coffee-houses like Brightman's near Wapping Old Stairs, Ive's in St Bartholomew's-lane, Oliver's at Westminster Hall, Roe's at the Bridge-foot and the Admiralty Coffee-house over and against Whitehall.'

Solomon's Balms

Samuel Solomon sold a miraculous compound called Balm of Gilead. It was a proprietary brand of a preparation that had circulated widely in various versions in the eighteenth century. 'Its composition,' Solomon said, 'has been sanctioned by the most learned physicians of the age. It has preserved its reputation from the period prior to the birth of Christ, growing in Gilead in Judea in 1730 BC.'

Indeed the 'balm of Gilead' is mentioned twice in the Old Testament. It was medicine extracted from the balsam fir used in antiquity, though it is now used to refer to the buds of a species of North American poplar used to make cough syrup. Solomon had started life as a door-to-door salesman for 'Black Ball' boot polish. He claimed to have brought the balm to England via 'secret correspondence with the Honourable East India Company'. His version seems of have consisted of sage, mace and rosemary, mixed with turpentine and flavoured with lemon. He wrote:

> Among eastern nations, it has long been a favourite and popular remedy taken internally in cases of diseases of the intestines, ulcers of the lungs, liver and kidneys. Egyptian women possess the wonderful art of rendering themselves fruitful, either by the internal use of the balm, or perfuming their bodies with it. The beauty of the skin is said to be not

a little improved by it, and the ladies of the seraglio anoint their bodies with it after a tepid bath.

Solomon claimed that the Balm had been used by Frederick the Great to cure General Foquet and that it cured the yellow fever in the outbreak in the Americas. It also cured 'weak and shattered constitutions, hypochondria, horrors of the mind, sexual debility, intemperance, debauchery, inattention to the necessary care of health, luxury or studious life'. If it made Egyptian women fruitful, while the women of the seraglio splashed it all over – and it cured 'sexual debility' and 'debauchery' simultaneously – it had to be hot stuff.

A small bottle cost 11 shillings (55p), but you could get a family-sized bottle for 33 shillings (£1.65). Then you could get a crate containing three bottles for £5 for those disorders that had 'been for many years in proceeding to such a degree of

malignancy as cannot be eradicated in a few weeks'. These could be obtained, along with Abstergent Lotion and Detergent Oitment, from one of the House of Solomon's 400 outlets in England. There were 16 more in America and agencies sprung up in Quebec, Nassau and Bengal. On top of this Solomon provided a personal service. He could be consulted for the 'usual compliment of a pound note', or give advice in writing for just ten shillings and sixpence (53p). Dr Solomon became extremely wealthy.

One stern critic sought to discredit Solomon by publicly dosing a pig with Balm of Gilead. The pig did not enjoy the experience. It 'yelled most hideously while the medicine was poured down its throat, and afterwards ran about as if mad, endeavouring to bite everything with its reach – in a few minutes it lay down and continued to grunt most piteously until it fell fast asleep'.

Solomon also sold Cordial or Anti-Impetignes Balm of Gold, which he said contained 'no other mineral than gold, "pure virgin gold" and the "true balm of Mecca". He wrote about it in a book, which went into 65 editions.

The Cordial Balm of Gold, he said, was

... the real pure essence of gold, together with some materia medica. The process is long and laborious and not a single drop can be produced under nine weeks digestion, and the elements of which it is composed are only obtained with still greater labour, being extracted from the seed of gold, which our alchemists and philosophers have so long sought after in vain.

It seems to have consisted largely of brandy.

A number of tradesmen in Everton found that their wives had become drunkards after dosing themselves with the Balm of Gold. They decided to take their revenge on Solomon, who was a well-known figure in his hometown of Liverpool, where he advertised his wares by carrying a gold-headed cane on his daily promenade. One night they sent a messenger to his ostentatious house in the suburbs, asking him to come and attend a patient who lived a little way out in the country, and to be sure to bring several bottles of his celebrated Balm with him. Disguised in cowhides with the tails still attached, they hid behind a hedge and waylaid him on the road. Solomon mistook them for devils and was terrified. He sank to his knees and begged for mercy. His attackers then forced him to drink the bottles of his own Balm, ducked him in a pond and tossed him in blanket.

Daffy's Elixir

One of the most popular remedies of the eighteenth century was *Elixir Salutis*, also known as Daffy's Elixir, as the Reverend Thomas Daffy, rector of Redmile, Leicestershire, had devised it in around 1666. It was thought to have been made from jalap, sienna, caraway seeds, aniseed and juniper berries, soaked in alcohol and mixed with water and treacle. This sweet concoction was a powerful laxative and, presumably, got you drunk.

After the Reverend Daffy died in 1680, his daughter Katherine Daffy continued making the Elixir. The Elixir was sold at the Hand and Pen in Maiden Lane, Covent Garden; by Mr John Waters, a perfumer at the Naked Boy and Orange Tree, near the Maypole in the Strand; and in many coffee houses.

Katherine Daffy was not the only one making the Elixir. In 1709, John Harrison of Prujeans Court in the Old Bailey 'charged Mrs Elizabeth Daffy with making invidious remarks on his *Elixir Salutis*'. She had said that he had taken the 'house in Prujeans Court clandestinely and with pretending to be her husband's assistant in preparing the Elixir'.

Harrison defended himself by saying that 'he knew the secret sometime before the death of his father, Dr Anthony Daffy, which he presumes was before the said Elias Daffy was privy to the preparing of the said Elixir (he being then a Cambridge scholar) and the same was communicated to him in the year 1684, at the time when he was going to travel beyond the sea'. Harrison also asserted: 'I am well assured that those who have tried mine will apply themselves to nobody else for *Elixir Salutis*.'

Bottles were sold with a wrapping that claimed: 'The Elixir was much recommended to the public by Dr King, physician to King Charles II, and the late learned and ingenious Dr Radcliffe.' Charles II had, of course, died in 1685.

In 1708, Nicholas Boone was selling Daffy's Elixir in Boston, Massachusetts, at the sign of the Bible near the corner of School-House Lane, and advertised the stuff in the *Boston News-Letter*. A half-pint bottle fetched four shillings and sixpence (£25 in today's money). Daffy's Elixir was still on the market as late as 1759.

Goddard's Drops

In the seventeenth century there was a great vogue for Goddard's Drops. Their inventor, Dr Jonathan Goddard, who was the professor of medicine at Gresham College and a fellow of the Royal Society, sold their secret to Charles II for £6,000 (£685,000 in today's money). It then came out that these drops were, pharmaceutically, similar in action to '*sal volatile*' – volatile salts – a preparation of ammonium carbonate used as a restorative in fainting fits. They later became known as smelling salts.

Lady Moor's Drops

Mr Wells, who lived against the Blew Bell in Long Acre near Drury Lane, sold 'Lady Moor's Drops' and claimed to be 'the only one that hath the true receipt from the Lady's son'. He said the drops 'never fail in curing consumptions, dropsies and all manner of coughs'. They also cured more colourful complaints. 'When people look yellow, black, green, or of several other sickly colours, by taking these drops they'll look for the future of a young, brisk and lively complexion.'

Oyl

In old England, linseed was frequently used as a cure for coughs and colds. One J.L. sold it at various coffee houses in the City. 'The Right, New, Cold-Drawn Linseed-oyl, which is so famous for the distempers, phthisick [pulmonary consumption], colds, and the only remedy for the plurisie, is drawn by J.L.,' said his handbill.

Also on sale was 'British Oyl', and Mrs Morton sold 'Strong Rock Oyl' at the Blew Bodice in Long-walk near Christchurch Hospital. Her oil cured bruises, contusions, gout, rheumatism, broken bones and the king's evil. Fifty or sixty drops of the oil taken in ale, wine or with sugar were an antidote to poisons, while 'Madamois- 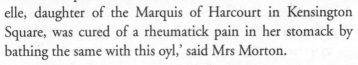 elle, daughter of the Marquis of Harcourt in Kensington Square, was cured of a rheumatick pain in her stomack by bathing the same with this oyl,' said Mrs Morton.

Vegetable oil elixir

An 'illustrious Spanish doctor' named Don Lopus, working in London, recommended his 'most inestimable vegetable and highly valued oil', which he claimed was so much in demand that 'my six servants are not able to make so fast as it is fetched away from my lodging by gentlemen of your city'. The reason for this is simple. 'For what avails your rich man to have his magazines stuft with Moscadelles [Muscadelles] of the purest grape, when his physicians prescribe him on the pain of death to drink nothing but water cocted with aniseeds?'

The oil was called Oglio del Scoto, which means 'oil of the Scottish' in Italian – which is odd as our man was from Saragossa.

Don Lopus also sold an amazing powder for the ladies. His sales pitch ran:

Here is a powder, concealed in this paper, of which, if I should speak to the worth, 9,000 volumes were but as one page, that page as a line, that line as a world, so short is this pilgrimage of man to the expressing of it. I will only tell you, it is the powder that made Venus a goddess, given to her by Apollo, that kept her perpetually young, cleared her wrinkles, firmed her gums, filled her skin, coloured her hair; from her derived to Helen and at the sack of Troy lost till now. In this our age it was as happily recovered by a studious antiquary out of some ruins of Asia, who sent a moiety [half] of it to the court of France, wherewith ladies there now colour their hair. The rest at this present remains with me, extracted to a quintessence, so that whenever it but touches in youth it perpetually preserves, in age restores the complexion, seats your teeth did they dance like virginal Jacks firm as a wall and makes them white as ivory that were black as hell.

The infallible cure

Morandi's Chocolate House in Playhouse Yard, Drury Lane, sold 'Sovereign Julep', prepared from a recipe by the Italian alchemist Giovanni Francesco Borri. It was 'an infallible cure for consumptions, ptisick, asthmas, catarrhs and all other distempers whatever afflicting the lungs. Morandi's handbill explained that:

> ... the 'Sovereign Julep' is universally esteemed in most parts of Europe as well as the whole world, as being first made and rightly prepared by that most eminent physician Shavillier Borri, lately deceas'd. A nobleman in his travels got the Receipt [from the aforesaid Shavillier] for the benefit of his

country; but lately coming to England, has not only here generously given it, as a mark of his favour to a particular friend, but has also taught him how to make the same.

Despite the nobleman's generosity and the fact that it did not save Signor Borri, a bottle of Sovereign Julep went for half a crown – that's 25p, or £25 in today's money.

Tar water

The famous philosopher, scientist and Anglican bishop George Berkeley (1685–1753) claimed that tar water – that is, water mixed with tar, allowed to stand then poured off – cured hysteria, gout, scurvy, piles, gangrene, smallpox, plague and 'all diseases of the urinary tract'.

In 1744 he published *Siris, a Chain of Philosophical Reflections and Enquiries on the Virtues of Tar Water*. The 'Siris' here is thought to conjure the dark, healing waters of the Nile. Not only did tar water cure these conditions, but it could also be used as a prophylactic. 'To sailors and all seafaring persons who are subject to scorbutic [scurvy-related] disorders and putrid fevers, especially on long southern voyages, I am persuaded that tar water would be very beneficial.'

Similarly, 'studious persons, also pent up in narrow holes, breathing bad air and stooping over their books, are much to be pitied. As they are debarred free use of air and exercise, this [tar water] I will venture to recommend as the best succedaneum to both.'

To the womenfolk he recommended: 'This same tar water will also give charitable relief to the ladies, who want it more than the parish poor; being many of them never able to make a good meal and sitting pale, puny and forbidden like ghosts at their own table, victims of vapours and indigestion.'

Live to 115

In his 1743 medical directory *Hermippus Recidivus: Or, the Sage's Triumph Over Old Age and the Grave*, John Cohausen maintained that it was possible to live to 115 in good health simply by inhaling the 'salubrious vapours' given off in the breath of young girls. Their perspiration was also good, so for medicinal purposes, 'he caused some of these young people to lie with him'.

A similar treatment worked for women:

What is more common than to see a woman advanced in years grow not only brisk and lively, but strong and healthy, by marrying a young husband. She drinks his breath, exhales in spirits, extracts his moisture, and thereby invigorates herself, while the poor man suffers from the impure contagion of her breath and vapours, and, from the malignity of this ill-chosen union, sinks very quickly into apparent weakness, and falls at last to what the common people call a galloping consumption. Strange, that the death of a young man should result from his marriage with an old woman, and that the taking of a young wife should repair the waste and prolong the life of an old man.

CHAPTER SIX

Pills and Powders

 S WELL AS ELIXIRS AND DROPS, pills and powders were widely available. They had similar miraculous properties.

Blomfield's pills

Obviously it saved time and money if you could take one pill that cured everything and one Mr Blomfield did a roaring trade with was his *Pilulae in Omnes Morbus* or 'Pills against all Diseases'. He published testimonials to prove just how effective they were. One of these came from Chichester and was dated 19th of the 11th month 1677 – this would have been 19 January 1678 as, until the *Calendar (New Style)* Act of 1750, the year began on 25 March, not 1 January. It read:

> These are to acquaint thee with a remarkable cure that hath been lately performed with thy pills up to daughter of Edmund Stevens of the Parish of Appledrum near this city. She hath been extremely afflicted with tormenting pains

in her stomack and many times in her limbs, very much loathing her meat, not being in a capacity to eat with her father and her mother at their table in several years. Much hath been spent upon physicians and in physick for her cure, but all in vain.

She is now cured with taking thy pills, and hath continued in good health since last spring. I might inform thee of several others, but having nor order for it by those cured, shall say no more at present.

Blomfield lodged at the Blew Balls in Plow Yard in Fetter Lane, but his pills could be obtained from 'Mr John Painter at his house called John's Coffee-house, above the Royal Exchange in Corn-hil'; Mr John Bayns, tin-man at Bird cage in Cock-lane end against Holborn Conduit; Mr Flaxmore at the Maiden Head near Cherry-garden stairs in Redrif-wall; and Mr Edward Chandler, shoemaker, at Old Bedlam Gate going into Moorfields.'

Golden Vatican Pills

Doctor Trigg sold his 'Golden Vatican Pills' from his house on Tower Wharf. His handbill urged the reader 'be not so injurious to thyself as presently to commit this paper to the worst of offices'. I assume he means wipe your arse with it or throw it down the privy. 'It designs thy good, therefore first read (three minutes perform the task) after which use thy discretion.'

As usual, these pills cured everything from ague to scurvy. Also: 'They will keep their virtues many years, even the age of man. They may be conveyed to any plantation without the least danger of decay, and are made up in tin boxes and sealed with the doctor's own seal, containing twenty for two shillings.'

Normally the formulae for these patent medicines are kept a closely guarded secret, but the recipe for Vatican Pills came to light in a seventeenth-century manuscript. It read:

Take, anise, mastich, ginger, cardamoms, cinnamon, zedoary, mace, cloves, saffron, aloes wood, turbith, manna, senna, mirabolams, of each one drachm [sixteenth of an ounce], rhubarb one ounce, aloes two ounces, scordium half drachm. Mass with syrup of roses. Smith, an apothecary at the sign of the Three Black Lions in the Old Bailey makes them.

These ingredients are exotic fruits, herbs, roots and resins, which are largely laxatives or traditional antidotes to poison.

Never Failing Pills

An 'expert operator' living at the 'signe of the Red Ball in Bartholomew Close, with two black posts at the door, near unto Smithfield-gate' made 'Never Failing Pills'. He said:

My 'Never Failing Pills' are so prepared that the tenderest patient may take them. They are excellent good of seamen to take to sea with them, for they keep their full vertue for seven years. A private lodging may be had if required, and the house is so private, that no notice can be taken of your coming to him, from six in the morning until ten at night.

His handbill also warned about other 'ignorant pretenders... [who] will use you as unmerciful and they are unskilful'.

Health-Procuring Pill

John Hooker of St Paul's Chain near Doctors Commons had a 'Grand Balsamick and Health-Procuring and Preserving Pill' which he declared to be the 'most pleasant in the world'. From his handbill, it is clear that it was a hangover cure that also claimed other miraculous properties. The handbill read:

It is a compound of the most costly and precious ingredients that ever art or nature yielded, and is adapted to all ages and constitutions. Among other truly remarkable properties, it draws away the corroding humours from the lungs, and by that means surceases the toothache. It fortifies the optick nerves and by that means preserves and strengthens the sight.

Nor is it less beneficial to purge away the dregs of unconcocted wine, which occasions morning nauseousness of the stomack, the decay of appetite, and that Scottish dulness attends hard drinking.

Peasouper lozenges

There was no universal cure for the London fog, but in the seventeenth century 'The Famed and True Lozenges of Blois' were a popular remedy for the coughs and colds it caused. 'The salt and sulphurous vapours particularly in London,' said the handbill, 'joined with a foggy and moist air which begets rheums and coughs, lead many learned physicians to seek divers remedies, amongst which the particular preparation of the juice of licorish is rightly called the True Balsam of the Lungs.'

The Unlearned Alchymist pills

In 1662, Richard Mathew published a books called *The Unlearned Alchymist, his Antidote, or a Full and Ample Explanation of My Pill.* The pill was the antidote to all poisons. 'A gentleman who drank two hundred grains of opium at one draught, then swallowed a pill yet is in good health,' declared Mathew. It was further claimed:

This pill corrects all vegetable poysons, so that any exceeding portions is hereby moderated. Likewise it corrects all poisonous qualities in man's body, and expels them if they be curable; it helpeth agues (if the direction in my book be followed) also all fevers, headach, tooth-ache, dries up dropping rhumes, catarrhs which destroy the lungs: Presently helpeth all colds, cough or surfeits; it removes pains of the breast, trembling of the heart, cleanseth the blood, helpeth fits of sudden swooning and convulsions. Drunk with white wine, it cleanseth the reins and kidneys of gravel, openeth the urinary passages, drives out the stone, oft times with the urine, sends forth matter, with jags like paper or cloth of sundry colours; also by vomit, like clots of flesh, or baked blood, breaks inward imposthumations to astonishment; it eases all griefs and pains, aches got by colds, surfeits or bruises, whereby many secret and hidden griefs cured which otherwise could not be discovered. Also this pill used according to the directions given in my book, will speed and ease helpeth the French pox: If it be effectively used, cures some kind of gouts, and doth ease the pain of the most malign, brings quiet rest. It helpeth the shaking or trembling of the joints, palsie, dropsie, pleurisies. Strengthens the brain and memory, revives and comforts the heart above any cordial in the world. Brings the monthly course, whether they be wanting or abounding. It is the present help for any kind of flux for blood, or otherwise, by siege or uriters, and stops them incontinently. It strengthens and opens the spleen, tears away wind in an incredible manner. I know no distemper it doth not ease or cure.

Unfortunately, the pills did not help Mathew, and in 1662 his widow was selling them. She dismissed the claim that 'my husband put jollop' – a powerful purgative – 'and such-like in his pills'. To prove this she published his recipe:

They consist of the best tartar, saltpeter, heated together in an iron kettle, stirred well and allowed to cool. This salt is then mixed with oyl of turpentine, and allowed to stand for six months, then the opium and hellebire added, the whole then well beaten into a paste with a little more turpentine.

Scots Pills

Old Scotland had some curious cures too. One of the most popular was the Scots Pills developed by Dr Patrick Anderson, a well-known physician of the Stuart era. In 1635 he published a treatise on his pills, whose formula he said he had acquired in Venice. If you want to make some at home, take 12 ounces of Barbados aloes, half an ounce of colocynth and half an ounce of gamboge. These must be ground into a very fine powder, then beaten with two ounces of soap, a little water and three fluid ounces of oil of anise, and divided into three-grain pills.

After Dr Anderson died, his daughter Katherine continued making his pills. In 1686 she transferred the not-so-secret formula by deed to a surgeon in Edinburgh named Thomas Weir, who patented it the following year. However, rivals began to appear south of the border. In a handbill Mrs Isabella Inglish claimed that their Majesties – William and Mary – had authorised her to make and sell them at the Hand and Pen near the King's Bagnio in Long Acre. Mrs Inglish insists that 'she alone makes Dr Anderson's Grana Angelica or the famous true Scots Pills and no other are genuine'.

She was particularly critical of a Mr Mogson, who 'pretends to have the receipt form Mrs Katherine Anderson, and hath had the impudence to counterfeit my printed directions verbatim. Nor can he make appear he was ever in Scotland as he pretends.'

Another person peddling Anderson's Scots Pills in old England was John Gray of the Golden Head, between the Little Turnstile and the Bull Inn in High Holborn. He claimed to make the pills 'according to the doctor's method during his life-time'. In 1699 his pills fetched five shillings a box, which was sealed with his coat of arms in red wax. It must have been comforting for the patient to see printed on the box, the words: 'Remember you must die'.

Another piece of off-putting packaging was found on Robert Rotherams 'Elixir of Balmen and Mint' which he sold at the Golden Ball in Sweetings Alley in Cornhill, near the Royal Exchange, in 1678. He claimed that it would 'quicken all the faculties of nature, make a cheerful heart and lively countenance; each glass being sealed with the Bleeding Pelican'.

In 1703 the 'true Pills' were on sale at Old Man's Coffee-house at Charing Cross. And in 1711 Mr Lewis was selling Anderson's Scots Pills at the Blew Ball in Little Bridges Street and Russell Street in Covent Garden, declaring that they 'are the nicest thing in the world to sweeten, purifie, and cleanse the blood and of great use to sea-men, travellers and fast-livers'.

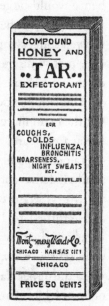

Lewis had a number of other curious cures on offer. There was a 'comforting stomack plaister for coughs, colds and wheesings. 'Tis worn by several persons as a stomacher all the winter for a preservation.' He had his own version of Daffy's *Elixir Salutis*, 'richly prepared with Venice treacle, the greatest preservative that art or natural can suggest'. Then there was 'true Friars Balsam, sufficiently known to the Nobility and Gentry, which has gained the reputation of the greatest Balsamick in the world. 'Twas never published 'till now, but has been kept by the Gentry, who were at the expense of making it as a closet jewel. Sold in flint bottles at ten shillings each.'

Ward's Pill and Drop

In the eighteenth century, Joshua Ward made a fortune from a patent medicine that came in pill and liquid form – even though it killed those who took it.

A 'drysalter' by trade – that is, a dealer in drugs, dyestuffs, gums and products needed in the arts – he was returned as Member of Parliament for Marlborough in 1716, although he had received not a single vote. One of two rival mayors – and hence would-be returning officers – filled in his name on the writ. Unseated the following year, he fled to France, where he showed some sympathy for the Jacobite cause and was said to have met some monks who gave him the recipe for the medicines that became known as Ward's Pill and Ward's Drop.

The composition of these remedies varied over the years, but the main ingredients of the Pill were dragon's blood, sweet Malaga wine and antimony, a well-known poison. The Drop contained mercury, aluminium chloride and nitric acid, a similarly lethal concoction.

In 1733 Ward obtained a pardon for his Jacobite dealings and returned to England. He advertised his Pill and Drop widely in the newspapers, claiming they cured gout, rheumatism, scurvy, palsy, syphilis, scrofula and cancer. He also cultivated the upper classes. A young maidservant in the household of Lord Chief Baron James Reynolds named Mary Betts, who had been ill for some time, was 'on Whit Sunday suddenly struck with a dead palsy'. Her periods stopped. She had 'not only emaciated to the degree of a skeleton, but had entirely lost all muscular motion, insomuch that whenever she found herself inclined to sleep, her nurse was obliged to pull down her eyelids and to raise them again whenever she was disposed of to wake'. The 26-year-old maid was 'left by the doctors as absolutely incurable'.

After a dose or two of Ward's remedy, the young woman vomited and sweated profusely, and was 'with difficulty kept alive'. But the treatment 'brought down the menses'. Soon she was up and about, dressed herself unassisted and walked in the garden. Before long she could 'manage her needle and had a good appetite and digestion'. Today, her illness would be diagnosed as a psychosomatic condition, brought on by an unwanted pregnancy. As it was, it gained Ward's Pill and Drop a valuable testimonial.

When George II had a painful thumb, his doctors diagnosed gout, but were unable to cure him. Eventually he called for Ward, who spotted that the thumb was, in fact, dislocated. While examining the thumb, he gave it a sudden wrench. The

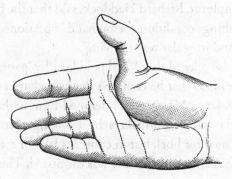

king cursed and kicked him on the shins. Once the king had calmed down, Ward asked him to move his thumb. He did and found that the pain had gone.

Ward's reward was the use of an apartment in Whitehall and permission to drive through St James's Park. He could now claim royal patronage and went on to treat Princess Caroline for her rheumatism with his Pill.

However, in 1734 the *Grub Street Journal* reported the case of a Mrs Gilbert, landlady of the Horseshoe Alehouse in Essex Street, who took one of his pills. She vomited 34 times, purged her bowels 22 times and 'died miserably' the following night. Ward was blamed, but got Jane Clerke of the Golden Cup in Drake Street, one of the barmaids at the Horseshoe, to swear an affidavit that Mrs Gilbert was a 'gross, fat woman' with an umbilical hernia. When she had taken Ward's cure, she said she felt 'much better for it'. But then she had 'supped on a hock of bacon and greens'. The printed directions that came with Ward's medicine forbade patients drinking milk or eating greens.

There were other casualties. Hester Straps, a barmaid at the 'Bagnio, near Charing Cross' died after taking Ward's Drop. But her employer, Richard Haddock, said that she had been in a 'languishing condition beforehand occasioned by hard drinking and irregular way of living'.

It was also alleged that Ward paid healthy 'patients' to pretend to be ill, so that he could be shown to have cured them. The *Gentleman's Magazine* condemned him as the friend of undertakers and coffin-makers by bringing them so much trade. He sued for libel, but in court his lack of medical qualification came out and the case was dismissed. This, however, did his reputation little harm. The writer Horace Walpole testified to Ward's ability to cure headaches. He wrote to Sir Henry Moore: 'I don't know what to say about Ward's medicines because the cures he does are performed by him in person. He rubs his hands with some preparation and holds it on your forehead, from which several have found instant relief.'

Novelist Henry Fielding commended him for his selfless work for the poor after he converted three houses near St James's Park into a hospital for the needy. And he nursed the 12-year-old Edward Gibbon through a life-threatening illness, allowing him to go on to write *The Decline and Fall of the Roman Empire*. It is therefore not so easy to dismiss Ward as a quack.

Ward came with up a new method of manufacturing sulphuric acid at a fraction of its former price and gave generously to charity. When he died in 1762, he left £2,000 (£225,000 in today's money) to his niece and £100 (£11,000) to his coachman.

The English fashion powder

The Sun in Gutter Lane near Cheapside was a popular haunt for doctors in the seventeenth century. R.F. Philatethes sold 'a Chymical Powder called the 'Metallick Eagle'. There is, he said, 'not the like medicine extant, unless the Grand Medicine of the Philosophers, and I know not any that dares to the pretend to have obtained it yet'.

Fletcher's Powder was also on sale at the Sun in Gutter Lane in 1679. 'It powerfully cures that disease, *A la mode d'Engleterre*, with all its symptoms, and there is nothing able to withstand its power, against all other diseases but against death.' Fletcher explained how it worked:

> It is a medicine of a Solar (or Gold like) nature made by Art most subtile, penetrable and capable by it splendid beam, to dispel those mists in the air, which cloud and darken the Sun of the little world of man; and he that hath such medicine as this, need not so much mind the uncertain indications, diagnosticks and the like verbal impertinences, which serve only ostentation.

The powder was recommended for 'madness, inflammation of the brain and all violent pains of the head', especially when a spoonful was taken with 'wine, ale, beer, sider or mead'. It may also 'save life at sea when the doctor's chest fails'. You could obtain it from 'Captain Newman at his Coffee-house in Talbot Court, in Grace-church-street; Mr Blunt at the Black Raven, over against Bedford House, and Mr Jer. Howes, Scrivener, near the Spittle in Bishops-gate-street'.

Powdered mummy

In the seventeenth century powdered mummy was sold as a cure-all for everything from asthma to poisoning. Paracelsus was particularly keen. The best mummies, he said, came from criminals who had been hanged as from them you could get a 'gentle siccation that expungeth the watery humour, without destroying the oil and spiritual which is cherished by the heavenly luminaries and strengthened continually by the affluence of the impulses of the celestial spirits'.

The use of powdered mummy went into decline as people found they could not bear the pain and vomiting it induced. But the healing power of the dead was not lost completely to old England. In Manchester in Victorian times, a woman asked for a pinch of clay from a priest's grave to ward off epilepsy in her children.

CHAPTER SEVEN

Dubious Devices

 UMANKIND HAS LONG sought daft devices to cure its ills. In past times these were merely talismans that worked by sympathetic magic. But as scientific knowledge grew, they became more and more sophisticated.

Magnets and mummies

Paracelsus was convinced of the curative powers of magnets and one of his cures says: 'Take a magnet impregnated with mummy.' Once you have got your mummified magnet, you were to 'sow some seeds that have a congruity with disease'. The idea here was to stroke the patient's affected parts with the magnet, and then bury it with some seeds. As the seeds germinated and grew, the patient would get better.

Lodestones

In the Middle Ages, lodestones were sold as aphrodisiacs. By the eighteenth century, Henry Hind Pelly, of Upton, Essex, wore 'constantly a piece of lodestone, sewed in a little flannel case, suspended by a black ribbon around his neck next to his skin'. He was a gentleman of advanced years, so this was not designed to turn him on or arouse the womenfolk of his acquaintance. Rather, he had read in an old book that a lodestone warded off gout. He had even gone to the trouble of obtaining 'one of the most powerful in the world, lodestone occurring in Golconda [southern India], and effected a successful cure for his troublesome illness'.

Rings

Gold rings through the ears were thought to ward off diseases of the eyes, which explains why chavs can see so well. Rubbing the eyeball with a spouse's gold wedding ring was thought to be a cure for sties. Rings of various type were also supposed to protect the wearer against arthritis, strokes, cramp, epilepsy and palsy.

In the eighteenth century, it was thought that you could cure fits with a silver ring forged by an unmarried silversmith and made out of five silver sixpences collected from five bachelors. Henry VIII, it seems, went one better. It is thought that he wore a cure-all ring made out of metal from coffin hinges.

Edward the Confessor gave one of his rings to a beggar. It was returned some years later. By that time it had gained a reputation for curing the 'cramp and falling sickness' – epilepsy. Later, special rings were struck to be given away as amulets on Good Friday by Henry VIII and Queen Mary.

Colour cure

Red was thought to be a therapeutic colour because it symbolised warmth. Red bedclothes would be used to treat smallpox as they were thought to draw the pustules to the surface. Edward II's doctor, John of Gaddesden – who gets an honorary mention in the prologue to *The Canterbury Tales* – treated the king's son this way. The prince was cured so completely that he was not even scarred.

The Saxons had a remedy that involved wrapping a shrew in a red rag, while a strip of red silk with nine knots in it tied around the neck was thought to stop a nosebleed. This cure migrated to the West Indies, where a piece of scarlet cloth worn around the neck was used to ward off whooping cough.

The Lee-Penny

Sir Walter Scott, the Scottish writer famous for *Rob Roy* and *Ivanhoe*, also wrote a novel called *The Talisman*, published in 1825. The book is about a magical coin, the Lee-Penny, a dark red, heart-shaped stone set in the back of a silver groat of Edward IV's reign. According to tradition, the stone was brought to Scotland in the fourteenth century by Sir Simon Lockhart Lee from the Holy Land, where it had been used to cure fever and other ailments.

To unlock its powers, the Lee-Penny was drawn once around a vessel filled with water and then dipped three times into the liquid. In an 'Account of the Penny in the Lee', written in 1702, the penny was then 'taken and put into the end of a cloven stick, and washen in a tub full of water, and given to cattell to drink, infallibly cures almost all manner of diseases' and 'the people come from all airts of the kingdom with their diseased beasts'.

In the year 1629 the 'routting ewill, a strange and suddane diseas' hit Scotland, 'quhairthrow' an ox 'was nevir able to ly down, bot routted continuallie till he deid'. To cure this disease people travelled from East Lothian 'to the laird of Ley is house and cravett the len' of 'his cureing stane – quhilk was refuisit be the lady; but [she] gave thame ane certaine quantitie of water in flaccones quhairin the said stane was dippit, quhilk being gevin as drink to the bestiall haillit

thame'. However, the church took a dim view of this and they had to do penance in the kirk at Dunbar. In mitigation they pleaded that this was the ordinary practice of 'husbandmen of the best soirt'.

The Lee-Penny also worked south of the border. During one of the epidemics of the plague that hit Newcastle in the reign of Charles I, the city fathers borrowed the Penny, although they had to deposit a bond of £6,000 for its safe return. It is said that, 'such was their belief in its virtues, and the good that it effected, that they offered to forfeit the money and keep the charm-stone'.

There is talk of another silver piece called the Lockerbie Penny, which is supposed to be kept at Lockerbie in Dumfriesshire. When used for the cure of madness in cattle, 'it is put in a cleft stick, and a well is stirred round with it, after which the water is bottled off and given to any animal so affected'.

Tractors

One of the curious cures of late eighteenth-century England came from America, brought to London by Connecticut-born Benjamin Douglas Perkins, who set up home in the former home of the famous surgeon John Hunter at 18 Leicester Square. He brought with him metal 'tractors' invented by his father Elisha. These were a pair of metal rods, sharp at one end, rounded at the other. When they were drawn across the skin they would cure just about anything.

Perkins published a book in which he claimed that one of the rods was made out of copper, zinc and gold; the other out of silver and platinum. The rods sold for five guineas (£370 in today's money). It seems that they were actually made out of brass and iron and cost just sixpence to make. But they came in a handsome red Morocco case that could be 'carried with perfect convenience in the waistcoat pocket'. Hundreds of pairs were sold. The Royal Society accepted a pair as a gift and their use became widespread in high society.

But Perkins was not content for the rich alone to benefit from his cure. In 1803 he set up the Perkinean Institution in Frith Street, Soho, to dispense healing to the poor. Its president was Lord Rivers and among its list of distinguished vice-presidents was Benjamin Franklin's son. A second branch of the institution was opened in Durham under the patronage of the Bishop of St Davids.

The following year, Perkins claimed that details of over 5,000 cures using his tractors had been published. For each published case, he said, some 300 other cases had been treated successfully, but had gone undocumented – so the amazing Perkins's tractors had already produced a million and a half cures, that is around one for every seven people living in Britain at the time.

Perkins then turned the healing properties of his tractors on pets and farm animals. According to his handbill – which warned that counterfeiting the instructions for the use of the tractors was a felony,

> . . . the tractors had been found a safe, speedy and effectual remedy in the following disorders: acute and chronic rheumatism, including lumbago and sciatica, gout, sprains, contusions, burns, scalds, inflammations of the eyes; also of

the skin, as erysipelas and tetters; painful inflammatory tumours, as biles and whitlows; violent spasmodic convulsions; as epileptic fits, cramp and lock jaw; pleurisy; stings and bites of venomous insects; fluor albus; pains in the head, face, teeth, ears, breast, side, back, limbs, and all analogous diseases of the horse.

Not everyone was convinced. Dr John Haygarth of Bath made tractors out of wood and painted them to look like the original metal ones. Then he sent these out to other general practitioners, who were soon reporting remarkable cures with them. This burst the bubble. Perkins packed his bags and returned to New England £10,000 the richer.

Anti-Rheumatic Towel

In Victorian times, you could save yourself from the pain of 'rheumatism, neuralgia, constipation, indigestion and liver complaints' simply by having a quick rub down after a bath with Bellhouse's patent Anti-Rheumatic Towel.

Riding room

In 1867 the Prince of Wales and the Emperor of Austria endorsed Vigor's Horse Action Saddler. This was a mechanical horse that you could ride in the drawing room. It claimed to cure hysteria, gout, poor circulation, insomnia, rheumatism, dyspepsia and liver problems without, the *Lancet* said, 'the expense and difficulty of riding a live horse'.

Electric Brushes

In 1872 Dr Scott's Electric Brush promised to cure baldness, along with headaches, nervousness, biliousness, dandruff and grey hair – provided only one person used it. If pattern baldness ran in the family, each family member would have to get their own brush.

Meanwhile, the Electro-Magnet Brush promised to end sleepless nights, softening of the brain, paralysis, exhaustion of the nervous system, rheumatism, skin disease, neuralgia, functional diseases of the heart, mental despondency, loss of muscular or nerve power, nervous headaches, kidney disease, dyspepsia and catarrh. 'As lightning purifies the air, so must electricity purify the blood,' the advert said. It was a 'joy to invalids', a 'substitute for medicine' and 'human life was prolonged by its use' – by 'imbuing the human organism with new life, health and strength, and developing and invigorating the brain'.

While the Electro-Magnetic Hair Brush stimulated the roots with 540 currents of electricity which 'often brings out a fine growth of hair on bald heads', the Electro-Magnetic Flesh Brush used 704 currents to invigorate other parts of the body.

Carbolic Smoke Ball

On 30 October 1889, Fredrick Augustus Roe applied to the London Patent Office for a patent on his Carbolic Smoke Ball. According to the application, this was a 'hollow ball or receptacle of India rubber or other suitable elastic material, having an orifice or nozzle provided with a porous or perforated disc or diaphragm consisting of muslin, silk, wire or gauze, perforated sheet metal or the like, through which, when the ball is compressed, the powder will be forced in a cloud of infinitesimally small particles resembling smoke'.

The powder was carbolic acid. Illustrations show ladies of distinction pumping the artificial smoke up their nostrils.

The Carbolic Smoke Ball Company of 27 Princess Street, Hanover Square, claimed that it could cure everything from hay fever and whooping cough to 'throat deafness', and it was on the market when an influenza epidemic hit Britain in 1891. The price of the ball was ten shillings (50p), post-free. Refills were five shillings. A Mrs Carhill read the advertisement and bought a Smoke Ball from a local chemist. She used it as directed three times a day from 20 November 1891 to 17 January 1892, when she promptly came down with the flu. She asked for her £100 reward, but the company refused to pay it. In a landmark decision on 6 December 1892, the appeal court found against the company. It was forced to pay up.

Mrs Carhill lived on until she was 96, when she died of old age and flu. Mr Roe went on to design horse and dog versions of the Carbolic Smoke Ball. He also patented a device for grooming horses and designed sprung horseshoes for a smoother ride.

The idea that the inhaling of noxious fumes was good for you persisted. In the early twentieth century breathing in fumes from the gasworks or the acrid vapour of bitumen from road tar was thought to 'open the lungs' as effectively as a trip to the seaside.

CHAPTER EIGHT

Plagues and Pestilence

 LD ENGLAND WAS RAKED by epidemics. The Black Death struck in 1348, killing nearly half the population. It returned regularly up until the Great Plague of London of 1664 and 1665, which resulted in some 75,000 deaths in a total population of around 460,000. Travellers brought fevers and agues back and tuberculosis haunted the slums.

Plague

In 1577 a vicar in London said in a sermon that the cause of the plague was sin, particularly the performance of plays on the public stage. As a result, when the plague hit, the theatres were closed. Houses where people were infected were marked with the Greek letter tau, traditionally the last letter in the Hebrew alphabet, or the headless St Anthony's Cross, a habit brought over from France. Later the words 'Lord have mercy on us' were added under the sign.

The first major hospital for the treatment of contagious

diseases was built on three acres of land in London by St Bartholomew's Hospital. It was paid for by the capture of a Spanish treasure ship by Sir Walter Raleigh in 1593.

Common protection against the plague

At the time, the best protection again the plague was thought to be onions, whose smell was believed to purify the air in ten days. The treatment for cholera was drinking rhubarb juice if you were rich, or rose-hip syrup if you were poor. The use of rose-hip syrups as a pick-me-up for children continues to this day.

The Green Dragon Tavern on Cheapside sold a beer – 'an Excellent Electuary' – that warded off the plague. It cost sixpence a pint – a lot of money in 1665. This was probably a better way of reconciling yourself to your fate than the Royal College of Physicians' cure. They recommended pressing roasted onions stuffed with treacle and figs against the buboes. Treacle itself was thought to be effective.

Toads were also popular. Dried over an open fire and pressed against the swollen lymph glands, they were thought to draw out the disease. Dried, powdered toad was a popular ingredient in many medicines, or you could make your own by simmering a toad in milk.

At times of plague, most doctors fled to the countryside. Those who stayed in the city wore strange masks with long beaks filled with herbs that they breathed through. The eyeholes were filled with thick glass to keep the miasmas or plague-ridden air out. They also wore platform soles to save them from stepping in anything infectious, and were clad in thick leather dresses. The outfit was completed by a white stick, which was used to beat away those infected but not confined to their houses.

It was thought you were safest if you lived in a house sheltered from the wind and stayed indoors with the windows closed. Eating fish, waterfowl, poultry or beef was best avoided. Nothing should be cooked in rainwater and the use of olive oil was thought to be fatal. Exercise, sleeping during the day and, of course, bathing should be avoided at all costs. But the most drastic cure of all was attempting to catch syphilis, which was thought to ward off the plague.

Otherwise you just had to keep your pecker up. The contemplation of gold and precious stones was said to be 'comforting to the heart'. In the fourteenth century, people were advised not to think about death. Thoughts should be directed to 'pleasing and agreeable and delicious things' – ornate gardens, pleasant landscapes and elevating music.

Fumigation

When the Black Death arrived in England, Edward III ordered the Mayor of London to 'cause the city to be cleaned from all bad smells, so that no more people will die from such smells'. Elsewhere they fired cannon to clear the air. Saltpetre and brimstone were burned on fires in the hope that the acrid smoke produced would act as a fumigant. Bedclothes would be aired in the fumes. Later, gunpowder was also burnt as doctors recommended fumigation twice a day. Children as young as three were encouraged to smoke tobacco to keep the plague at bay. Boys at Eton College were beaten for failing to smoke during the Great Plague, although it is not clear whether the beating or the smoking was supposed to be efficacious.

A French doctor claimed that his fumigation, which comprised saltpetre, sulphur and amber, had proved successful in Toulouse, Lyons and Paris. 'Angier's Fume', as it was called, was soon in great demand, and the secretary of state Lord Arlington and the privy council ordered the Lord Mayor and aldermen of London to: 'Give Angier all encouragement and distribute his medicaments.'

Other strong smells were brought into the fray. People would carry nosegays of herbs and flowers pressed against their noses. Daniel Defoe wrote about a woman who snorted vinegar and washed her head in it. There was a run on vinegar in 1665.

Plague pills

There were, of course, 'Infallible preventive Pills against the Plague'. These competed with 'The only True Plague Water' and 'The Sovereign Cordial against the corruption of the Air'. Indeed, there were so many cures doing the rounds that, in 1666, 'A list of the preservatives and medicines against the plague that were mostly used' was published at the 'sign of the Angell, neere the Great Conduit in Cheap-side'. The author recommended:

As preservatives against the disease, eate every morning as much as the kernell of a nut of this electuarie, which I shall keep always ready for you, or of treacle mixed with conserves of roses or diascordium [a strong-smelling plant], the quantitie of two white peas.

Let your chambers be ayred morning and evening with good fires, wherein put juniper, frankincense, storax [the balsam of a bark of an Asian tree], bay leaves, vinegar, rose water, rosin [pine resin], turpentine, pitch, tarre or some of them.

When you go abroad, chew in your mouth the root of angelica, gentian, zedoarie, enula campane or the like. Likewise twice a week, take a scrupell of the 'Pestilenciall Pill', in two pills, when you go to bed or an hour before supper.

Also I have prepared tablets to wear about the neck, of which I did see great aid and experience the last great sickness, as also Pomanders to smell to.

As remedies after a person is infected, after bleeding, mithridatum [dogtooth violet taken as an antidote], one dramme and a halfe; of the best London treacle one dramme, and mix with them Carduus benedictus or Angelica or Scabious Waters.

Sometimes the cure sounds worse than the disease.

Eliminating agues

The ague was a fever, marked by chills and sweating, that recurred at intervals. It was known in England since the fourteenth century. Most commonly associated with malaria, it would have been brought back by travellers.

There were, however, various strange ways to prevent disease in the first place. In Sussex, a necklace made from wood chips from a gallows was used to prevent the ague, although a man's woollen sock filled with earthworms could be worn instead.

Eels were also good against the ague. The seventeenth-century medical man Sir Kenelm Digby recommended cutting the nails of the sufferer, and putting the parings in a bag. This was to be hung around the neck of a live eel. The eel was then placed in a tub of water. 'The eel will die,' said Sir Kenelm, 'the patient will recover.'

The right foot of a black dog hung over the right arm would do as well. In medieval Kent the contents of a horse's hoof were boiled in water as a cure for the ague.

In eighteenth-century Sussex, it was recommended that you fast for seven days, eating only seven sage leaves. Or you could swallow woodlice rolled up into balls, which were known as 'pill-bugs'. Swallowing a live spider would do as well. Some preferred to keep the spider in a bag hung around the neck, which, as we have seen, was a cure for the whooping cough in Norfolk.

The Norfolk parson and diarist James Woodforde (1740–1803) had a more robust cure for the ague. He recorded that when a feverish relative came to stay: 'I gave him a dram of gin at the beginning of the fit and pushed him headlong into one of my ponds, then ordered him to bed immediately.'

Fever powder

In the eighteenth century, fever was particularly rife and it came in numerous varieties. There were nervous fevers, putrid fevers, inflammatory fevers, remittent fevers, intermittent fevers, simple continued fevers...

Fortunately, there was a remedy that was universally acclaimed called Dr James's Fever Powder. It was found to be effective not just against fever but also against rheumatism, sore throats, pleurisy, colds, catarrh, measles and inflammatory diseases. In general it was found to slow the progress of the condition and limit its duration. The powder came in packets costing two shillings and nine pence (14p) and £2.

Among its devotees were Horace Walpole and Oliver Goldsmith. Walpole swore that he would keep on taking it even if the house were on fire. When Goldsmith died of the purple fever, Walpole maintained that he would have recovered if he had kept on taking Dr James's cure, rather than reverting to conventional medicine.

According to an advertisement in *Bell's Weekly Messenger* of Sunday, 26 June 1831, the good doctor also provided Analeptic Pills. As well as stimulating the central nervous system, these were supposed to excite natural secretions to ease complaints of the stomach and bowels, biliousness, indigestion, febrile and gouty affections and rheumatism, along with other 'chronic diseases'. The remedy was sold in boxes costing four shillings and six pence (23p) and £2.

Jesuit's Bark

Cinchona – originally known as Peruvian or Jesuit's Bark – was introduced to England from South America in about 1658. It contained quinine and was undoubtedly a useful remedy for fever.

It was sold under various proprietary names, one of which was 'Phanchimagogum Febrifugum'. The powdered bark was divided into doses wrapped in paper. These came with the directions:

> You must take it all at once, that is one sealed paper, in the pap of a roasted apple, as big as a hazel nut; before you rise in the morning fasting, and within one hour after, drink some posset-drink [hot, sweetened and spiced milk cuddled with ale or wine] or some broth made of fresh meat or fresh butter, and then keep your bed for three hours, if you wish to be cured of all kinds of Tertian Agues or other Intermittent fevers. All the operation of it is done in three hours.

This remedy will keep good during the whole life of a man.

One Dr Saffold, the tributary of the College of Physicians, made more extravagant claims for the bark.

It infallibly cures the stone, dropsie and gout, taken inwardly and outwardly, rubb'd on the gums it hastens the cutting of the teeth. It cures convulsions, botts [colic], kib'd heels [chilblains on the heel], farcy [respiratory ulcers], chilblains, corns, the mange, spasms, also religious and love melancholy, meazle in swine, Christians and prating in elderly persons, and makes an admirable beauty water.

It was sold at Physicians' Hall at three shillings an ounce.

Cures for consumption

Tuberculosis, formerly known as consumption, was a killer from ancient times onwards and there were, of course, numerous interesting cures for it. One was a chicken stew made from pieces of chicken flattened with a club, dates and herbs. Pearls and gold had to be added and the whole thing cooked in a pot inside a bigger pot. Oh, and the chicken – a cock – had to be torn to pieces while it was still alive. If you were too squeamish for that you could swallow slugs.

The leaves of various herbs were also recommended. But these could not be picked by human hand. The plant had to be tied to the leg of a dog or a cock, so it would be uprooted when the animal pulled away. The juice of the leaves then had to be consumed every Wednesday morning and the rest of the plant burnt. In Scotland being passed through a wreath of woodbine would cure the consumptive.

Dairy products were thought to have great healing powers, particularly the milk and butter of cows left to graze in a churchyard. Even the sanatoriums set up in the nineteenth and early twentieth centuries went along with this, force-feeding their inmates 16 glasses of milk and a dozen eggs a day. Some took the more radical approach that sucking on the breasts of a healthy woman was the cure.

The riding cure

The famous seventeenth-century doctor Thomas Sydenham claimed that horse riding was the cure for consumption. The consumptive poet John Keats was hoisted on to a horse for a canter. He was dead at 25.

The art of healing

In 1827 Irish artist John St John Long (1798–1834) claimed to have found a cure for consumption and set up a clinic in

Harley Street. The cure involved rubbing a special medicine on the chest of the patient and salving any irritation caused with cabbage leaves. He soon had a celebrity following. However, when a young Irish girl called Katherine Cashin underwent the treatment her skin became inflamed and, soon after, she died. Charged with manslaughter, Long turned up at the Old Bailey with a crowd of his supporters. Nevertheless, the jury found him guilty and he was fined £250, which he paid there and then in cash.

Surprisingly, this did not put him out of business. The following year, another patient died. This time he was acquitted. Three years later he died himself at the age of 36, of TB, no doubt contracted from one of his patients. He left the secret of his cure for consumption – which he valued at £10,000 – to his brother.

Cabbages and cures

In the nineteenth century, those suffering from consumption were told to use cabbage leaves to cure the wan look of the skin that the disease caused. Perhaps fortunately, there was no way that they could be applied to the lungs, which are the seat of the disease.

For the disease itself and other chest complaints, garlic was thought to be successful. Science has since confirmed that chemicals contained in garlic are effective.

CHAPTER NINE

A Little of What You Fancy

T HAS LONG BEEN THOUGHT that a medicine must taste awful if it is going make you better. On the other hand, a little of what you fancy does you good and substances that we now take for pleasure or as part of the daily round were once thought to have remarkable healing properties.

The virtues of coffee

London's first coffee house was opened in 1652 in St Michael's Alley, Cornhill. Its proprietor Pasque Rosee, from Ragusa, now Dubrovnik in Croatia, published a handbill describing the 'Vertue of the Coffee Drink'. In it he recommended drying the berries in an oven, grinding them into a fine power, then boiling them in spring water. Half a pint should be drunk, not after eating, but half an hour before. He said:

> It is a very too good help to digestion, quickens the spirits and is good against sore eyes. Is good against headache,

helpeth consumptions and the cough of the lungs. It is also excellent to prevent dropsy, gout and scurvy, and will prevent drowsiness and make one fit for business.

It could be bought in his coffee house, he said, 'at the sign of his own head'.

Caffeine

Decaf would do you no good. *The Lady's World* of 1898 recommended 'Bishop's Citrate of Caffeine' for businessmen, students and ladies of leisure 'prostrated by the excitement of shopping and sight-seeing'.

Tea

Tea was first advertised in England in 1658 in the monthly publication *Mercurius Politicus*, which extolled the 'excellent and by all physitians approved Chinese drink called Tcha, by other nations Tay or Tee, sold at Sultaners Head Cophee-house in Sweeting's-Rents by the Royal Exchange'.

Soon after 'the volatile spirit of bohee-tea' – black tea from the Wu-i hills north of Fuhkien, the first type brought to England – was recommended in a handbill as:

> . . . the most absolute cure for consumptions, and all other decays of nature whatsoever incident to mankind; being infinitely more Balsamick and healing to the lungs than the common infusion of the leaf in water.
>
> It is likewise a very rich cordial for clearing the heart when oppress'd with melancholy and vapours. This spirit, the first of its kind that was ever made in England, mix'd with punch makes one of the most agreeable liquors in the world.
>
> It is also a special antidote against any infection of the air and if 15 drops be taken going to bed in a glass of spring water, it never faileth to procure a sound sleep. It is sold at two shillings and sixpence a bottle at Batson's Coffee-house against the Royal Exchange and at no other place.

Later, Garraway's Coffee-house sold tea as 'a cure for all disorders' at from 16 to 50 shillings a pound.

Tobacco

The health-giving properties of tobacco were long known. The seventeenth-century herbalist Nicholas Culpeper detailed them in his Complete Herbal:

> It is found by good experience to be available to expectorate tough phlegm from the stomach, chest, and lungs. The juice thereof made into a syrup, or the distilled water of the herb drank with some sugar, or without, if you will, or the

smoak taken by a pipe, as is usual, but fainting, helps to expel worms in the stomach and belly, and to ease the pains in the head, or megrim, and the griping pains in the bowels. It is profitable for those that are troubled with the stone in the kidneys, both to ease the pains by provoking urine, and also to expel gravel and the stone engendered therein, and hath been found very effectual to expel windiness, and other humours, which cause the strangling of the mother [womb]. The seed thereof is very effectual to expel the tooth ache, and the ashes of the burnt herb to cleanse the gums, and make the teeth white. The herb bruised and applied to the place grieved with the king's evil, helps it in nine or ten days effectually.

Monardus [a contemporary doctor in Seville] saith, It is a counter poison against the biting of any venomous creature, the herb also being outwardly applied to the hurt place. The distilled water is often given with some sugar before the fit of an ague, to lessen it, and take it away in three or four times using.

If the distilled faeces of the herb, having been bruised before the distillation, and not distilled dry, be set in warm dung for fourteen days, and afterwards be hung in a bag in a wine cellar, the liquor that distills therefrom is singularly good to use in cramps, aches, the gout and sciatica, and to heal itches, scabs, and running ulcers, cankers, and all foul sores whatsoever.

The juice is also good for all the said griefs, and likewise to kill lice in children's heads. The green herb bruised and applied to any green wounds, cures any fresh wound or cut whatsoever: and the juice put into old sores, both cleanses and heals them. There is also made hereof a singularly good salve to help imposthumes, hard tumours, and other swellings by blows and falls.

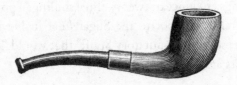

As already mentioned, a tobacco-smoke enema was supposed to revive the drowned. Finely powdered tobacco was used as a disinfectant and, when the plague broke out in London, it was thought that smokers were less likely to catch it.

However, there was the downside. As early as 1761, the English physician John Hill first described tobacco-induced cancer. His patient had cancer of the nose. Moreover in 1851, the surgeon James Paget warned a patient with a white patch on his tongue where his pipe rested – known as a 'smoker's patch' – that he would certainly get cancer of the tongue if he continued smoking.

Snuff

Like tobacco, snuff was used for medicinal purposes when it first became popular in England in the seventeenth century. In 1706 the 'best Oragare, fine Burgamot, Tongar, Germany and Itallian snuffs at two shillings and one shilling an ounce [and] the best Spanish, Havana and Sevile snuffs were sold at five shillings a pound... as a present remedy for the most violentest headache or toothache, and as infallible curers of coughs or ptsicks, and a preventer of those distempers'.

Mr Harrison at the West End of the Royal Exchange sold 'Lisbon snuff, strongly recommended to improve the eyesight', at six shillings an ounce or twenty-three shillings a pound. And Edwyn Salter, next door to the Sugar Loaf in Nevill's Alley, Fetter Lane, sold a 'Sternutatory Snuff' that would 'fortify the brain and its animal faculties'.

Opium

Opium came into widespread use in England in the eighteenth century. When the 'quicksilver doctor' Thomas Dover was not poisoning people with mercury, he was prescribing Dover's Powders, which contained opium. Initially prescribed for gout, it quickly became another cure-all. Dover's Powders comprised ten grains each of opium, the Brazilian root ipecacuanha and potassium sulphate. This was a powerful emetic and may well have saved Dover's patients from the effects of the other things he prescribed for them.

Later, a patented version of Dover's Powders was made from a mixture of ipecacuanha and opium. This analgesic-cum-sedative relieved pain and induced sweating. It was particularly effective in cases of diarrhoea, and was still in use in the 1970s.

Dover's mentor Thomas Sydenham – the man behind the 'riding cure' for consumptives (see page 105) – invented laudanum, which was opium dissolved in alcohol, a double whammy if ever there was one. Dr Johnson's wife Tetty was an addict. It was considered too powerful for children – because of the alcohol, not the opium. Instead they were given syrup cordials laced with opium as a cure for stomach ache, teething pains and sleeplessness. Brews with such names as Godfrey's Cordial, Mrs Winslow's Soothing Syrup, Mother's Friend or Quietness were found to keep the little darlings in a contented, drug-induce haze.

But then opium had the royal seal of approval. George III used it regularly and his son, the Prince Regent, guzzled down cherry brandy laced with laudanum.

As if laudanum was not powerful enough, Dr J. Collis Browne added morphine, cannabis and the sedative-hypnotic drug chloral hydrate to the mixture to produce a cure for influenza, coughs, colds, catarrh, asthma, bronchitis, neuralgia, gout, toothache, rheumatism, diarrhoea, stomach chills and other bowel complaints. With Dr J. Collis Browne's Chlorodyne, you felt no pain – and it was much cheaper than going to the doctor.

Cocaine

The peoples of South America have long used the leaves of the coca plant to increase their physical endurance. The Spanish conquistadors were impressed. In 1860 the active ingredient was isolated and it was used as a local anaesthetic. Cocaine toothache drops were soon on the market and cocaine was used as a hay fever cure – ironically it rid the user's nose of that stuffed-up feeling.

Otherwise, its general invigorating properties were not overlooked. Queen Victoria, Robert Louis Stephenson and US President William McKinley all imbibed wine laced with coca, while explorer Ernest Shackleton set out across the icy wastes of Antarctica fuelled by pills call 'Forced March'. Made from coca leaves and kola nuts, these pills, it was said, could 'allay hunger and prolong the power of endurance'.

French writer Emile Zola endorsed a proprietary brand of Queen Victoria's tipple called Vin Mariani. He called it: 'The elixir of life, which combats human debility, the one real cause of every ill – a veritable scientific fountain of youth, which, in giving vigour, health and energy, would create an entirely new and superior race.'

The list of conditions Vin Mariani cured was impressive: nervous trouble, throat and lung diseases, dyspepsia, consumption, malaria, the grippe, wasting diseases and general debility. It was also a tonic for the body, nerves and brain for overworked men, delicate women and sickly children. Press advertisements for the wine said that emperors, empresses, princes, cardinals, archbishops and other distinguished personages endorsed it.

Alcohol

By the age of 20, Dublin-born doctor Robert Bentley Todd had already been appointed professor of physiology and general morbid anatomy at King's College London and had published the first book of his five-volume *Cylopaedia of Anatomy and Physiology*. Although a highly religious man, he was not caught up in the teetotal movement that was sweeping the country in the middle of the nineteenth century. Indeed, he was a great advocate of the use of alcohol in medical practice. 'Alcohol, in some form or other, is a remedy whose value can scarcely, I think, be overestimated,' he wrote, 'and upon which, when carefully administered, I rely on with the utmost confidence in a great number of cases of disease which are at all amenable to treatment.'

He retired after a distinguished career at King's in December 1859 due to ill health, and set up practice in Brook Street. Six weeks later he began vomiting blood. This continued for two days until in died on 30 January 1860. The post-mortem revealed an advanced case of cirrhosis of the liver.

The English un-Frenchified

Wine and brandy were common ingredients in most early medicines. The ancient Greeks used wine from Cyprus to extract the properties of certain drugs and, to this day, alcohol is used as a medium to administer chemicals.

In the seventeenth century, one of the most popular 'cordials' was called Lucatelli's Balsam. It contained olive oil, Venice turpentine, red sandalwood, or 'dragon's blood', balsam of Peru and rose water – all washed down with good Spanish wine.

Another popular wine-based remedy was Rose's 'Balsamick Elixir'. It was 'the most noble medicine that art can produce... its incomparable virtues being such that it gives or restores to nature what's wanting and takes away what's harmful. It is a signal restorative for consumptive persons and there is not such another preparation in the whole world....'

Better yet: '...It cures the English Frenchify'd beyond all the other medicines upon the face of the earth. It removes all pains in three or four doses and makes any man, tho' rotten as a pear, to be sound as a suckling lamb. Whoever tries it, on my word, shall have just reason to thank me as well as pay me.'

Lily the Pink

The Liverpool band The Scaffold had a number one hit with 'Lily the Pink' at Christmas 1968. In the song Lily was billed as: 'The saviour of the human race, For she invented medicinal compound, Most efficacious in every case'.

There was indeed such a person as Lily the Pink. Her name was Lydia E. Pinkham and she began advertising her Vegetable Compound in women's magazines in 1875. It was: 'A sure cure for *prolapsus uteri*, or falling of the womb, and all female weaknesses including leucorrhoea [a white discharge from the vagina], irregular and painful menstruation, inflammation and ulceration of the womb, flooding [don't ask]....' It was also efficacious for: 'all weaknesses of the generative organs of either sex, it is second to no remedy that has ever been seen before in public, and for all diseases of the kidneys it is the greatest remedy in the world'. According to the advertisement: '98 out of 100 women benefited'.

Readers were invited to write in for advice about their complaints. Mrs Pinkham would send a personal reply, which, naturally, advised the correspondent to consume large quantities of Vegetable Compound. This worked well enough until 1905, when the *Ladies Home Journal* published a picture of Lily's grave. Lily had sadly died in 1883.

Accused of fraud, the company that made Vegetable Compound admitted that Mrs Pinkham had indeed died, but said that her daughter Jennie was answering the letters. This turned out not to be true either. The replies were in fact being generated by a typing pool. Then in 1906 a law was passed requiring all medicines to declare their ingredients on the label. Vegetable Compound turned out to be 15 per cent alcohol – a great deal stronger than most wines. That lost it the teetotal market and sales plummeted, although some people still swore by it.

CHAPTER TEN

The French Pox

HE FRENCH CALLED IT the Italian or Neapolitan disease. The Russians and Germans called it the Polish disease. The Arabs called it the disease of Christians, while the British and Italians blamed the French. This is because the French king Charles VIII had marched into Naples in 1495, a year after the first case of syphilis had been identified there, possibly brought back from the New World by one of Columbus's sailors. His soldiers were thought to have spread it to northern Europe as they retreated back up the Italian peninsula. On the other hand, the disease previously known as leprosy in Europe might actually have been syphilis. It was thought to spread by sexual contact, had hereditary features and responded to mercury.

Great Venus unmask'd

In his book of 1672, *Great Venus unmask'd*, Gideon Harvey recorded various theories about how syphilis had come about. Astrologists said that it had been caused by confusion in the heavens. Others said that the Spanish had put lepers' blood in wine in Greece to infect troops billeted there; while others still said a leper who had slept with a prostitute started it.

Harvey also recorded one of the earliest attempts to halt the epidemic. 'The Germans were of the opinion that feeding too oft upon Pease and Bacon might breed the pox, and therefore their magistrates forbad the selling of all sorts of Peas.' Harvey was not convinced. 'This opinion is so unreasonable that it needs no confutation,' he concluded.

The royal remedy

Towards the end of his life, Henry VIII suffered from so many complaints that it is not clear whether he had syphilis or not. But a man of his proclivities must surely have had a jolly good stab at catching it. As it was, he fancied himself as a doctor and came up with his own proprietary anti-syphilitic plaster, made from resin and powdered pearls.

Mercury: the main cure

The standard cure for syphilis until the twentieth century was mercury. This could be taken in the form of pills or injected – sometimes directly into the penis. It would also be mixed with pig's fat and acid and applied to the genitals. There are even reports of special underpants impregnated with mercury for continuous application. The results of taking mercury were fever, sweating, excessive salivation, sores in the nose and mouth, loss of teeth, bleeding gums and a foetid smell issuing from the patient – which should, at least, have ensured that the disease spread no further.

Culpeper's cock cure

An altogether more pleasant cure also found favour in the seventeenth century. A young cock – of the chicken variety – was to be boiled with spices and herbs, along with three ounces of young red worms collected from a horse's dunghill and cleansed in white wine. The resulting broth was to be mixed with crushed snails taken from a vineyard and applied as a poultice. Nicholas Culpeper also advised men with the clap to soothe their bits in the warm innards of a freshly killed fowl.

A variety of cures

Eighteenth-century London boasted numerous cures for syphilis – which was lucky as there was a lot of it about. The writer James Boswell (1740–95) was particularly enthusiastic about the ubiquitous Balm of Gilead.

Boswell also caught gonorrhoea some 19 times and tried curing it with bloodletting, purges and special diets. His favourite treatment, though, was Kennedy's Lisbon Diet

Drink, which was a mixture of sassafras, sarsaparilla, and liquorice. He downed two bottles a day at half a guinea a time.

Then there was Aqua Mirabilis, which was made from dried horse droppings mixed with vegetable oil. It cured palsy, dropsy and the plague, as well as all manner of venereal diseases.

For those caught out 'too often sporting in the Garden of Venus', as one handbill put it, there were Bateman's Drops and Velno's Vegetable Cure, although detractors warned that this made your limbs turn into plants. Restorative Electuary was 'a sovereign remedy for venereal complaints' and Leake's Genuine Pills were 'much used for curing venereal disease in a short time'.

Angel's disease

If you have a new and fashionable disease to cure, it is best to give it a more appealing name. A doctor who lived 'at the sign of the Water Tankard in Northumberland-alley in Fanchurch-street near Aldegate, there being pales before the window', took to calling the *Morbus gallicus* that was raging though London in the seventeenth century '*Affection Allamode*'.

The name *Morbus gallicus* comes from *Syphilis sive morbus gallicus*, the title of a medical poem by the Italian doctor Girolamo Fracastoro written in 1530, which first gave the name 'syphilis' to the disease. It also popularised the name 'the French pox'.

At the time it was ravaging London it was also known as *Morbus angelicus*, which can be translated as 'the angel's disease'.

Remedies for swelling

Naturally it was best to avoid reinfection while taking any of the patent cures on offer, so sex was out. Patients were warned to avoid lascivious thoughts, sights and situations, along with food of a stimulating nature. In dire cases, laudanum could be injected or mercurial ointment or camphorated oil rubbed into the penis to bring down any swelling.

Leeches were use to bring down swelling of the testicles, and bougies – metal retractors – were used to hold open the diseased urethra. However, Dr William Buchan, a fellow of the Royal College of Physicians, related the terrible tale of a man who had to open the passage with a knitting needle every time he needed to urinate.

Two in one

In 1767 the eminent British surgeon John Hunter made two holes in his genitals and rubbed in 'the matter of a gonorrhoea' – that is, the pus – in an inoculation experiment. Unfortunately, he had taken the sample from a patient who had both syphilis and gonorrhoea. Hunter came down with both conditions, but concluded that they were one and the same disease. It was only in 1793 that they were shown to be two separate afflictions.

Restoring lost parts

In 1796 Dr Buchan published *Observations Concerning the Prevention and Cure of the Venereal Disease*, which warned that while 'mercury will do wonders, it cannot restore lost parts'. He recorded examining a syphilitic patient 'half of whose whole face was eaten away and part of the brain laid bare'.

By then, it was generally thought that seamen who dropped anchor in many ports spread syphilis. Buchan noted that he was consulted by a sailor who 'was too complete a tar to pay any attention to his health'.

As a preventative measure, Buchan recommended cleanliness. Washing the genitals with water would help, but vinegar, honey, turpentine or lead could be added. The water in London was polluted at the time, so gentlemen preferred to wash their bits in beer, wine, punch or brandy. Some rakes thought it best to warm the liquor in their mouths first.

The emphasis on cleanliness in combating venereal disease continued for the nearly 250 years. The US *Medical Annual* of 1913 was particularly stringent. It recommended:

In those who have been exposed to infection the entire penis is scrubbed with liquid soap and water for several minutes, and then washed with mercuric perchloride lotions 1:2000. Abrasions are sprayed with hydrogen peroxide. Two urethral injections of argyrol (10%) are then given and retained for five minutes. The whole penis is then rubbed with 33% calomel ointment, which is kept on for several hours.

By that time potassium iodide had been introduced as a cure. In 1909 a preparation of arsenic marketed under the Salvarsan name was found to be effective, but it was only in 1943 that it was proved that penicillin could cure the disease.

Use of condoms

Of course, you could have avoided catching syphilis all along, thanks to a prophylactic device invented by the Italian anatomist Gabriello Fallopio, who had the Fallopian tubes named after him. In his groundbreaking book *Observationes anatomicae*, he named the placenta, the clitoris and the vagina. He was also an expert on two other orifices, the mouth and the ear, naming both the palate and the cochlea. In his spare time, Fallopio devised sheaths to halt the transmission of the sexually transmitted diseases endemic at the time. These were made from fish skins.

It is thought that prophylactic sheaths were introduced to England by a courtier of Charles II named Colonel Condum, or Cundum, when he returned after the Restoration in 1660, and he seems to have lent his name to them. By that time, the technology had moved on./Sheaths made from dried sheep's gut were sold at the Rummer near Covent Garden and at the Rose in Russell Street, which was a well-known meeting place during the Stuart era.

Perhaps it is not surprising that women soon got their hands on them. Famously, Mrs Philips made and sold 'implements of safety' at the Green Canister in Half-Moon Street near the Strand in the late seventeenth century. It is said that she had so many satisfied customers that she grew rich and retired. The demand for her services was too great. 'After ten years leaving off business, she had been prevailed on by her friends to re-assume the same,' said a handbill announcing her comeback.

Not only did she boast 35 years experience in condom making, but also she now advertised a wide range of skins and bladders, which were available wholesale to apothecaries, chemists and druggists. She also sold all sorts of perfumes, which must have upped condom usage in that largely unwashed age.

When Mrs Philips eventually died, the business at the Green Canister was carried on by Mary Perkins, who sold 'all sorts of fine machines, otherwise called "Cundums", and also washballs, soaps, essences, snuffs, cold cream, lipsalves, sealing wax and ladies black sticking-plaister'.

CHAPTER ELEVEN

Sexual Healing

HERE HAVE ALWAYS BEEN rich pickings in the sexual field for the medical man. The fertile want contraception. The infertile want babies. Those who can't get it up are desperate to do so, while those who can need to be forced, for the highest moral reasons, to keep it down.

Sneezing as contraception

The pharmacological work *De materia medica*, by the first-century physician Dioscorides, was still widely used in sixteenth-century England. For contraception, it recommends inserting pepper into the mouth of the uterus. This was a bit of sympathetic medicine as sneezing is not a bad way of expelling semen from the vagina. Otherwise, Dioscorides recommended only having sex during the first five days after menstruation, a method now known as 'Vatican roulette'. *De materia medica* also described the use of cannabis and opium.

The mysteries of reproduction

Until the Renaissance and, particularly, the anatomical drawings of Leonardo da Vinci, the internal workings of the sexual organs were a mystery. That old fallback Galen of Pergamon was no help, as his work in the arena did not give him much opportunity to work on women. While he refuted Plato's idea that the womb was an animal in its own right living an independent existence inside a woman's body, he put forward an equally strange theory – that it was, in fact, an inverted scrotum. This meant that it had its own 'seed', which, if it went unspent, would build up and cause hysteria.

Medieval anatomical drawings show the womb as a mysterious organ shaped like a cat's head filled with little men and women. Wombs in the Middle Ages were shown with seven chambers. The three on the left produce girls. The three on the right produce boys, while the middle one produces hermaphrodites.

Until the nineteenth century, it was thought that babies came from tiny men – homunculi – who lived in the testicles that were implanted in the womb, where they grew. They were born only when they had developed enough strength to climb out.

Cures for impotence

In the days before Viagra, there were other ways to help a man stiffen the sinews. Eating mint or chewing ash seeds was found to help, while passion could be incited in women with mandrake root or sage.

Dr Buchan recommended tonics of Peruvian bark or steel. The waters of Tunbridge Wells should also help, along with cold baths especially in salt water. But his best advice in the case of impotency was for every man to marry the woman he loved. 'When this is not the case, satiety and disgust will succeed,' he said, 'and the unhappy husband, in the vigour of life, may, by mistake, impute his want of ardour for connubial enjoyments to impotency.'

Electrical vigour

In the Victorian era the wonders of electricity became evident. Advertisements appeared for electric belts. Dr McLaughlin's Electro Vigour promised to restore the 'fire of life', as well as cure nervous disorders, a weak back, lumbago, rheumatism, stomach, liver, kidney and bowel troubles, 'come and go' pains and 'that tired feeling – after every other treatment has failed'. The muscle-bound model in an advertisement for the Supreme Electric Belt announced: 'I am a man once more.' As an add-on, these belts had 'suspensory sacks', which provided a tingling sensation to the testicles.

Happily, some of these electrical belts had no batteries or electrical current in them at all. Instead, the insides were covered with pepper and glue, which produced a tingle when the wearer put it on.

The Medical Battery Company – sometimes known as the Electropathic Institute – sold electric corsets designed by the aptly named C.B. Harness. Advertisements in the *Young Ladies Journal* in the 1890s showed thoughtful young ladies daringly stripped down to their corsets, which gave off sparks.

These devices cost just five shillings and sixpence (29p) or ten shillings and sixpence (53p) for two, so that 'ladies of all

ages and all stations of life' could 'procure at once one of Harness's beautifully designed and scientifically constructed electrical corsets'. They cured 'functional irregularities… hysteria, loss of appetite, dyspepsia' and 'internal complaints'. An electric corset 'invigorates the whole system' and was a boon to 'delicate women and all who suffer from organic diseases, rheumatic affections, and weak back. It will always do good, and never harm. There is no sensation felt whatever wearing it, while benefit always and quickly follows.' More importantly to the readers of the *Young Ladies Journal*, Mr Harness's electric corset also 'assists nature in the HEALTHY DEVELOP-MENT OF THE CHEST'.

Love potion for the over-eighties

Many seventeenth-century doctors' handbills made extravagant claims. However, the bill titled 'The Old Made Young' is not one of them. The author wrote:

> I will not pretend that I have known my great Restorer cure any distemper, excepting one, and such a one, as I believe

never was helped by any medicine but this, that is to say in LOVE AFFAIRS both in OLD MEN AND WOMEN.

This I suppose many will laugh at, and few will believe, but it has that miraculous operation that it renders old men and women of three or four score, as youthful as those of twenty or thirty years of age.

The ultimate sexual problem

The condition *penis captivus* was well known in medieval times. It was God's punishment for fornication among the owls and bats at night in churches and churchyards. The penis became trapped in the vagina and the embarrassed couple could only be separated at daybreak, with copious prayers and buckets of cold water.

The first case recorded by a doctor occurred in 1729, but the condition continued into the twentieth century. *Sexual Life of Our Time*, published in 1908, detailed a case in the Bremen docks: 'A couple were removed in a closed carriage, and taken to the hospital, and not until chloroform had been administered to the girl did the spasm pass off and free the man.' In another case two year later, ice had to be applied as well. After a similar incident in a Warsaw park in 1923 made the papers, the two young people involved shot themselves. The cause of the condition was thought to be a nervous spasm in the muscles of the vagina induced when the couple were caught at it in a public place.

The English confined their activities to the marriage bed, but cases were reported there too. One new bride in Victorian times had to go through an entire spring undergoing a course of treatment which involved 'the application of a probe, speculum, compressive sponge, glycerine tampons etc'. The doctor reported: 'The young and chronically neurotic woman grew every week more agitated and excitable so that she eventually responded to the smallest aggravation with compulsive crying fits.'

Incidents of *penis captivus* are now rare, though men sometimes get their foreskins caught on women's intrauterine devices. However, according to the *Journal of Urology*: 'Prolonged intercourse, particularly with the female subject in the superior position, and inadvertent flexion of the erect penis are well-described cases of penile trauma commonly leading to corporeal rupture.'

Fertility aids

Sex therapy and fertility clinics are not new. In 1780 James Graham, a medical man from Edinburgh, opened the Temple of Health in an elegant Adams' house in Adelphi Terrace in London's West End. While practising in Paris, he had meet Georgiana, Duchess of Devonshire, who he persuaded to come to London to open his fashionable clinic.

At the Temple of Health, Graham gave public lectures on his method of producing physical perfection in his patients. The entrance fee was two guineas and the hour-long talks were illustrated by a series of attractive young women – referred to merely as a 'Hebe Vestina' or the 'Goddess of Youth and Health' – who appeared in various states of undress. In his *Reminiscenes*, Henry Angelo, court-fencing master to George VI, recalled seeing the 'female who was lectured upon, who had no more clothing than Venus when she rose from the sea'.

Graham's advertisement for a new young lady to model déshabillé would read:

> Wanted genteel, decent, modest young woman; she must be personally agreeable, blooming, healthy, and sweet tempered and well recommended for modesty, good sense and steadiness. She is to live in the Physician's family, to be daily dressed in white silk robes with a rich rose coloured girdle. If she can sing, play on the harpsichord or speak French greater wages will be given. Enquire Dr Graham, Adelphi Temple.

One of those who applied and got the job was Emma Lyons. Whether she was genteel, decent and modest can be judged from the fact that, around that time, she was living with Captain – later Admiral – Payne and, soon after, with Sir Harry Featherstonehaugh. She certainly qualified physically as, according to a contemporary description, she had 'a perfect figure, fine regular features, and an indescribable charm and

attractiveness about her face and expression'. She later married Sir William Hamilton, becoming Lady Emma Hamilton, and was the mistress of Admiral Horatio Nelson.

Graham had met Benjamin Franklin both in America and Paris, and like him had studied electricity. He built a number of 'friction engines' that produced static electricity. This was used to shock his patients back into youth, vigour and health. Others were placed on a 'magnetic throne' or given mild shocks in the bath. More conventional treatments were also offered, such as milk baths and 'frictions'.

The main draw of the Temple, however, was the 'Celestial Bed'. This was made by a renowned tinsmith named Denton and was said to have cost Graham £10,000. It was in a separate room that could be reached by a private entrance. Graham himself left a description:

The Grand Celestial Bed, whose magical influences are now celebrated from pole to pole and from the rising to the setting of the sun, is twelve feet long and nine feet wide, supported by forty pillars of brilliant glass of the most exquisite workmanship, in richly variegated colours. The supercelestial dome of the bed, which contains the odoriferous, balmy and ethereal spices, odours and essences, which is the grand reservoir of those reviving invigorating influences which are exhaled by the breath of music and by the exhilarating forces of electrical fire, is covered on the other side with brilliant panes of looking-glass.

On the utmost summit of the dome are placed the exquisite figures of Cupid and Psyche, with a figure of Hymen [the Greek god of marriage] behind, with his torch flaming with electrical fire in one hand and with the other, supporting the celestial crown, sparkling over a pair of living turtle doves, on a little bed of roses.

The other elegant group of figures which sport on the top of the dome, having each of them musical instruments in their hands, which by the most expensive mechanism, breathe forth sound corresponding to their instruments, flutes, guitars, violins, clarinets, trumpets, horns, oboes, kettle drums, etc.

The post or pillars too, which support the grand dome are groups of musical instruments, golden pipes, etc., which in sweet concert breathe forth celestial sound, lulling the visions of Elysian joys.

At the head of the bed appears sparkling with electrical fire a great first commandment: 'BE FRUITFUL, MULTIPLY AND REPLENISH THE EARTH.' Under that is an elegant sweet-toned organ in front of which is a fine landscape of moving figures, priest and bride's procession entering the Temple of Hymen.

In the Celestial Bed no feather bed is employed but sometimes mattresses filled with sweet new wheat or oat straw mingled with balm, rose leaves, lavender flowers and oriental spices. The sheets are of the richest and softest silk, stained of various colours suited to the complexion. Pale green, rose colour, sky blue, white and purple, and are sweetly perfumed in oriental manner with the tudor rose, or with rich gums or balsams.

The chief principle of my Celestial Bed is produced by artificial lodestones. About 15 cwt of compound magnets are continually pouring forth in an ever-flowing circle.

The bed is constructed with a double frame, which moves on an axis or pivot and can be converted into an inclined plane.

Sometimes the mattresses are filled with the strongest, most springy hair, produced at vast expense from the tails of English stallions, which are elastic to the highest degree.

This bed, however, was not for having fun in. To Graham, fornication was as bad as masturbation. He said:

I must speak plainly gentlemen. Every act of self-pollution, every repetition of natural venery, with even the loveliest of the sex, to which appalled and exhausted nature is whipped and spurred by lust... is an earthquake, a blast, a deadly paralytic stroke to all the faculties of both soul and body. Blasting beauty, chilling, contracting and enfeebling the body, mind and memory.

He was against 'public prostitution' as it 'destroys the vigour of the genital parts, necessity tempting them to too frequent acts of venery'. Husbands and wives sleeping together were almost as bad. 'Nothing is more unnatural, nothing more indecent, than man and wife continuing pigging together in one and the same bed,' he said, 'and to sleep and snore and steam and do everything else indelicate together 365 times every year.' It was nothing short of 'matrimonial whoredom'. No, sex should be indulged in purely for the purposes of procreation. The Celestial Bed was for getting pregnant in.

> Any gentleman and his lady desirous of progeny, and wishing to spend an evening in the Celestial apartment, after coition may, by a complement of a £50 bank note be permitted to partake of the heavenly joys it affords by causing immediate conception, accompanied by the soft music. Superior ecstasy which the parties enjoy in the Celestial Bed is really astonishing and never before thought of in this world: the barren must certainly become fruitful when they are powerfully agitated in the delights of love.

There is some reason to believe that the Celestial Bed might have worked – not because of the magnets but because of the pivot mechanism. If the bed was tilted after sex so that the woman's feet were raised above her head, this would have aided conception as it would have retained the sperm in the vagina and helped it flow up towards the uterus.

Stuffing the mattress with the hair from stallions' tails was supposed to help by association – after all, stallions are thought to be particularly virile. The fact that the hair was very springy might have helped too.

Graham said that the cost of an evening on the Celestial Bed was £50, but Henry Angelo said that 'many a nobleman paid Graham £500 to draw the curtains'. It is not clear what extra service a nobleman would expect for this huge fee. However, one gentleman regularly in the audience at Graham's lectures developed 'a most marked predilection for the doctor's principal performer'. He found himself sorely disappointed when the Goddess of Health fell sick and died due, it was said, 'to a cold given by the damp sheets of the Celestial Bed'.

This, and a troublesome neighbour who fired pellets through open windows at the unfortunate nude models, forced Graham to move the Temple of Health and Hymen to Shomberg House in Pall Mall – an area then known for its brothels and sex shows. There, under the aegis of Mrs Hays, 'twelve beautiful nymphs, spotless virgins, would carry out the famous feast of Venus, as it is celebrated in Tahiti, with… twelve athletic youths' while twenty-three visitors of high standing, including five members of the House of Commons, looked on. Nearby Mrs Prendergast organised a *Bal d'Amour*, where dancers wearing only fig leaves were provided for guests to celebrate the 'Cyprian Goddess and her Rites'.

Graham dropped the price of his lectures to two shillings and sixpence during the day and five shillings at night. Attendance in the 'great Apollo chamber at the lecture and walking about the open apartments of this celestial paradise' rose to 1,000 a day. In his lectures, Graham railed against the debilitating effects of alcohol and the overuse of Spanish Fly. He also offered advice on overcoming impotence by detailing case histories. In one case, he mentioned a hairdresser who found himself impotent. However, one day, while dressing a particularly lovely woman's hair, the man was overcome by sexual desire. He downed tools and raced home to attend to his wife.

In another case, an elderly debauched woman found that she could not maintain a younger lover's interest. The cure, Graham said, was to take a lovely young woman to bed with them. Then, if her lover's ardour flagged, his mistress's nubile companion could reinspire his passion. It was necessary, Graham said, to 'tune body and mind for the most cordial enjoyment of prolific love'.

While Graham toured the country giving demonstrations, he became inflicted with a religious mania. On 3 April 1793, he signed an affidavit saying that 'from the last day of December 1792 to 15th day of January, 1793 he neither ate, drank, nor took anything but cold water, sustaining life by wearing cut-up turves against his naked body, and rubbing his limbs with his own nervous ethereal balsam'. This balsam was, naturally, on sale at the Temple of Health. Graham died the following year.

Sexual selection

Early in the seventeenth century, a Mr Lattese from Piedmont arrived in London claiming that, after 'a long series of experiments, he has discovered the wonderful secret of procreating either sex at the joint option of the parents. Should they desire to have a daughter, the success cannot be warranted with absolute certainty, but should they concur in their wishes to have a son, they may rely that by strictly conforming to a few easy and natural directions, they will positively have a boy.'

He claimed never to have failed in the 16 years he had made his 'Extraordinary Discovery'.

The indiscretions of youth

In 1795 William Brodum published *A Guide to Old Age and a Cure for the Indiscretions of Youth*. In it he related the tale of a youth of about 17 who 'devoted himself to seductive practise' and developed 'a swelling of the neck, and a convulsive motion in the extending muscles of the head… and eventual insensibility'. In this case, Brodum was called too late and the patient died.

However, in a similar case, Brodum effected a cure. A captain from the Indies who was about to get married approached him, labouring 'under a dreadful consumption and was apprehensive that matrimonial engagements would be detrimental to his health'. He said that, before he went to the Indies, he had been 'injured by a venereal disease'. However, on examination, Brodum could not find 'the least symptom of venereal taint', but there was evidence of 'that baleful habit to which he candidly acknowledged'. Brodum's Nervous Cordial had him completely cured within six weeks.

Another young lady 'fell into practises that she continued until she ran away with her music master at the age of 18. She had four children by her husband in three years, but they all died, as did the husband himself. Unfortunately she then took up her evil practices again until she remarried.' By this time her womb was already 'weak and slippery' and other doctors told her that she would have no more children. Again, with Nervous Cordial she was 'completely restored in a short time to a good state of health'.

Nervous Cordial was supplied in 'flint' bottles at five shillings and five pence (27p), eleven shillings and sixpence (57p) and one pound and two shillings (£1.10). It was available through eight outlets in London and through over sixty agencies across England, Wales and Scotland. There was also a five-guinea bottle that could 'only be obtained at the Doctor's House'.

Although there was no law against peddling patent medicines at the time, the Royal College of Physicians objected to Brodum advertising himself as 'Doctor'. But when he was hauled before the president of the Royal College and his censors, Brodum produced a medical diploma from Marischal College of the University of Aberdeen, which boasted among its distinguished alumni Samuel Solomon of Balm of Gilead fame. Asked how he had obtained the diploma, Brodum said that he had paid for it like everybody else.

Brodum kept the brass plate that announced him as Dr Brodum and now, in his advertising, maintained that his degree had been 'authenticated by the College of Physicians'. However, critics started a campaign against him, spreading the tale that a bottle of Nervous Cordial had been administered to a village ass, 'which on swallowing the dose, brayed most horribly… then fell down in a fit from which he was roused by throwing a pale of water full in its face, but had it not been for that emollient drench given by a skilful harrier, the animal would certainly have expired under the operation of the nostrum'.

Undeterred, Brodum continued advertising his Nervous Cordial and Botanical Syrup and went on publishing stories of his amazing cures until 1801.

Lowering the libido

Like many of his ilk, Nicholas Culpeper actively sought to lower the libido and recommended applying daisies to the genitals for the purpose, or eating lettuce.

Nocturnal emissions

These days we would not view a wet dream a medical problem, but it was considered so in the eighteenth century and Dr William Buchan's cure was drastic.

'The constitution is wasted by involuntary emissions during the night,' he wrote. 'I would recommend opium; from half a grain to a whole grain may be taken at bedtime. If this has not the desired effect, the dose may be increased to a grain and a half, or two grains. Its use out to be accompanied with tonics and corroborating medicines.'

However, there is a surer remedy. 'For the cure of unnatural pollutions, I always recommend matrimony. This, with regular living, and the use of the cold bath, seldom proves unsuccessful.'

The sin of Onan

Masturbation was another threat to health. In 1710 *Onania, Or the Heinous Sin of Self-Pollution and all its Frightful Consequences in Both Sexes Considered* was published. It was a bestseller of the age, with 15 more editions being printed over the next 20 years. Seven supplements were added and it was still rolling off the presses in 1759.

'Many young men who were strong and lusty before they gave themselves over to this vice have been worn out by it, and,' warned the anonymous author, 'without cough or spitting, dry and emaciated, sent to their graves.' They risked deforming their genitals to 'render them ridiculous to women'. Once they got over their laughter, their spouses would produce sickly children who, if they survived, would be 'always ailing and complaining: a misery to themselves, a dishonour to the human race and a scandal to their parents'.

Later, masturbation was thought to cause gonorrhoea, cancer, feeblemindedness, haemorrhoids, impotence, blindness, desiccation of the brain and, of course, death.

The cure for masturbation in the eighteenth century was dry food and thin gruel, avoiding anything that might cause wind. This comes from the old theory that an erection is caused by gases inflating the penis.

Bed was where danger lurked, so it was best to retire at night with turgid reading matter and not hang around in bed in the morning. Just in case, it was a good idea to tie a string around your neck and penis, so any movement below would wake you.

Meanwhile, women who indulged in masturbation would suffer 'hysterick fits'. They would grow pale or, otherwise, 'swarthy and haggard'. The cure was to refrain from the practice.

Spermatorrhoea

In the nineteenth century, the Victorians became obsessed with what they called 'spermatorrhoea' – the spontaneous and fruitless loss of sperm. More complex devices were developed to prevent it. There was a handy cap that fitted over the end of the penis, which was then chained to the pubic hair. The first stirrings of an erection would give the pubes a painful tug.

Stephenson's Spermatic Truss lashed down the penis with leather and canvas. There were devices with abrasive plates, but these worked less well as some sufferers found them stimulating – 'thereby tending much more to promote rather than prevent the disease which it is designed to cure'.

Dr Everett Flood sought to cure a youthful masturbator by encasing his hands in plaster. The ingenious Mr F. Orth developed a cooling system that detected an erection, then doused it with cold water and blasted it with cold air from a fan, causing even the hardest of hard-ons to wilt.

Some devices were positively gruesome. There were spermatorrhoeal rings with metal spikes pointing inwards, menacing even the slightest tumescence. Albert Todd's shocking solution was an electric cage suspended over the genitals from a belt. He also applied for a patent for a metal cylinder that fitted over the penis. To limit any 'longitudinal extension', it delivered a powerful electric shock. If the smell of burning flesh was too much for you, there was always the ultimate cure for onanism – castration.

Clitoridectomy

Female masturbation was also debilitating in Victorian times. In March 1866 the eminent gynaecologist Isaac Baker Brown published *On the Curability of certain forms of Insanity, Epilepsy, Catalepsy, and Hysteria in females*, in which he maintained that 'peripheral excitement of the pubic nerve' lead to hysteria, spinal irritation, epileptic fits, cataleptic fits, imbecility, mania and death. The cure, he maintained, was a clitoridectomy. 'I always prefer scissors,' said Mr Baker Brown, a fellow of the Royal College of Surgeons.

A number of Victorian women were mutilated this way, not

always voluntarily. But Baker Brown happily reported that those he had cured went on to get married and have children.

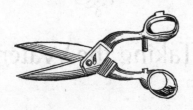

Women's problems

If a woman's period be 'obstructed' in any way – other than pregnancy – *The Family Physician* of 1794 recommends that 'proper means should be used to restore it: wholesome diet, generous liquors, cheerful company, and all manner of amusements'.

In the 1800s Dr A.I. Coffin brought medical botany to Britain in his *Botanic Guide to Health*, which sold 40,000 copies. In it he advocated juniper berries 'to promote monthly terms'. However, in *The Model Botanic Guide to Health* of 1893, the author William Fox, MD came up with a herbal cure: 'Pennyroyal is a favourite herb for female derangement, removing all obstructions arising from obstructed "perspiration".'

Meanwhile, for post-natal depression, *The Diseases of Females* of 1841 urged that 'the strait-waistcoat must be used without delay, if the patient cannot be cured without it'.

CHAPTER TWELVE

Taking the Waters

 ATER HAS ALWAYS been seen as pure and life giving – except in London, of course, where by drinking it you risked typhoid and cholera. However, good stuff could be brought in from outside.

Mineral water

The medicinal spring at Tunbridge in Kent was discovered in 1606 and the spa of Tunbridge Wells grew up in the seventeenth and eighteenth centuries. If, however, you wanted to take the health-giving waters but could not be bothered to travel all the way to Tunbridge, the apothecary John Coniers of Shoe Lane and later the White Lyon in Fleet Street had the answer – dehydrated mineral water. In a handbill dated 12 May 1679, he advertised 'an essence made of ye Minerall which quicklie you can make Tunbridge Waters. Any soft spring water mixt with a little thereof, becomes in nature a True Tunbridge Water of great use to those who desired to be spared ye journey to ye Wells.'

Purging water

The mineral spring at Epsom, which gave its name to the salts, was discovered in 1618. Later, another mineral spring was discovered closer to London. 'There is lately found out at Norwood in the Parish of Croyden in the County of Surrey, at Biggen Farm at Richard Jackson's, an excellent purging water which hath been approved by several eminent physitians of the Colledge and is found to be one of the best and gentlest purging waters that have yet been discovered,' ran the bill. 'You may have it at Mr Timothy Robert's, fishmonger at the Cheshire Cheese in Stock's Market, and at Mr John Hilliard's at the Strong Water Shop, over against Sir Thomas Lane's, near Milkstreet Market, London.'

Keeping clean

Old England was a filthy place. In the sixteenth century the court had to move regularly so the palaces could be cleaned, as courtiers would urinate and defecate pretty much where they pleased. Baths in palaces or in private homes were practically unknown. It was only in the late seventeenth century that public baths, or bagnios, were opened.

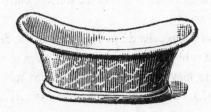

Duke's Bagnio

One of the first was Duke's Bagnio and Bath in Salisbury Stables, Long Acre. It was a hammam or Turkish bath along the lines of those common in the East, and in 1679 its owner, Sir William Jennings, received Charles II's patent 'for making all public bagnios and baths, either for sweating, bathing or washing'.

A handbill issued when Duke's opened described what the patron was in for:

Entering the hall, where the porter stands to take the money, you pass into a room furnished with a pair of scales, and thence into the dressing room with private boxes on each side, the middle walk of which is paved with black and white marble. This room is moderately warm. Then you pass into the bagnio, over which is a cupula supported by eight stone pillars within which you walk. This is paved with marble, the sides lined with white gally-tiles, and in the walls are ten seats as in the baths at Bath, with nitches, holding marble basins for washing.

On one side stands a very handsome pendulum clock to tell exactly how the time passes. Adjoining are four little round rooms, each about eight feet in size, of various temperatures and in each is a leaden cistern or bath, six feet long by two feet wide.

The visitor is received by the barbers in the dressing room and later a rubber brings him wooden clogs in exchange for slippers. He may then lounge or walk, or take a bottle of 'diaphoretick liquor [which makes you sweat]'.

After about an hour, his rubber dry-rubs him with a hair-chamolet glove, then having filled a cistern the patient lies in it, the water gradually being made colder.

Chamolet was a material said to be made from the hair of a camel, but usually the hair of the Angora goat was used.

The Duke's Bagnio was open six days a week. Two days were reserved for women; four for men. For VIP treatment there was a separate apartment with a large bath ten feet long, seven feet wide and five feet deep. This was filled with salt water.

Sweating house

There was another sweating house next door to the Black Bull in the Old Bailey 'where both men and women may be well accommodated at convenient seasons, being three days for men and three days for women'. Its bill spells out the health-giving properties: 'Sweating is as useful as bathing. It eases the pains in the limbs, opens the pores of the body, evacuates superfluous humours, cleanses the blood, prevents and cures the scurvy, and is most excellent in expelling those infections and venomous humours, and 'tis the best antidote in the world against all contagious distempers.'

Medical baths were available. 'In the same house there is a bath, for such as desire it, upon timely notice given, and this shall be artificially composed according to the necessity of the patients distemper requires.'

Medical services

There were other medical services on hand at the bagnio. At the Royal Bagnio in Newgate Street 'there is lately found out a good and clear water for bathing, and any persons that have no mind to may be cup'd either in the old way or according to the modern invention for two shillings and six pence'.

The 'modern invention' was one of the new scarifying machines with six or more spring-loaded blades to pierce the skin and Mr Wilcox, the Royal Bagnio's cupper, hired himself out freelance. His card had a picture of a Turk's head on it, as 'he now liveth at the Turk's Head in Newgate street over against Butcher-Hall-lane where he hath very good conveniences for sweating, bathing, shaving and cupping after the best manner'.

There were also women cuppers. 'At Canbury Cold Bath at Islington,' says one bill, 'Mary Lucas "cups" ladies at home and abroad whenever required. She hopes those ladies she has had the honour to guide at the last Mr Jones's Cold Bath in Newgate Street, will be pleased to employ her, and that those who have since honoured her with their favours, will continue to do so.'

Unisex and entertainment

The 'Sweating House' at the sign of the Black Prince in Duck Lane near West Smithfield offered a unisex service at competitive prices – 'all persons of both sexes may be sweated every Tuesday, Wednesday, Friday and Saturday, without fail. The price for men and women is one shilling and sixpence and those that are cupp'd the whole charge will be two shillings.'

It could also be visited privately. 'There is likewise a back door that comes into Bartholomew Close between the Chequer and the Red Ball where you will see over the door The Sweating and Cupping House.'

A surgeon named Henry Ayme kept the Queen's Bagnio in Long Acre. His handbill of 1706 says: 'The Queen's Bagnio is latterly beautified and divided into several rooms and is more convenient than before the reception of both sexes, where they may sweat and bathe every day in the week and be private to themselves.'

Of course, class was a factor in the choice of bathhouse. Ayme's bill continues: 'This bagnio is well known for to exceed all others, and to be more frequented by the Nobility and Gentry, by reason there is added a lesser bagnio of a lower rate for the diseased and meaner sort.'

You could just go there for a wash, though other facilities were provided. 'Those that desire may be bath'd without sweating either in cold or hot water, and cupt after the newest and easiest way with an instrument that scarifies all at once, with little or no pain, being the best of that kind ever yet invented. The price for one single person is five shillings, but if two come together, four shillings each.'

This was plainly encouraged. 'There is no entertainment for women after twelve of the clock at night,' the bill went on, 'but all gentlemen that desire beds may have them for two shillings a night for one single person, but if two lie together, three shillings both; which rooms and beds are fit for the entertainment of persons of the highest quality.'

Two persons together

In Drury Lane, London, there was the 'Hummums with Two Spikes before the door', where 'private sweating, bathing and fine cupping, after the new German manner were performed with greater ease than ever yet known with good and clean linen'.

The Germans used a single-bladed spring lancet to cut directly into the vein. The proprietor John Evans added: 'If any persons desires to the cupt in their chambers he will wait on them.' Otherwise, 'persons may sweat to what degree they please' and Evans boasted 'a diligent attendance of both sexes attending every day'.

'Likewise he had good conveniences for cold bathing, which was highly approved of all persons. The price for one person alone is three shillings, two persons together five shillings. Every person that comes single, hath a private apartment to him or herself. It is also accommodated with good lodgings for such as desire to lie all night.'

Little wonder, then, that the *Oxford English Dictionary* gives an alternative definition of 'bagnio' as 'a brothel'.

Chinese style

A variation on the Turkish system could be found at the China Hammam at New Red Lyon Street in Holborn, against Great Turnstile. Run by P. Brook, it provided:

> ... sweating and bathing both at once, after the China Manner, by a 'Dew Bath' without entering into water of heat of fire, or breathing the air wherein the body sweats. This is only performed by the heat and moisture of a continued warm vaporous dew or steam arising from decoctions of all sorts of drugs, as herbs, flowers, seeds, woods, waters, wines, etc., of various properties and qualities according to each one's occasion, which continually flowing and distilling on the body during all the time and is always preparing a new peculiarly for every one that uses it.

Water cure

Hydropathy had a brief vogue in Britain in the 1850s. The chief exponent was Dr Edward Johnson of, predictably, Malvern. He condemned 'drug practitioners' as 'doctors who dropped drugs of which they knew little into stomachs of which they knew less'. He and his sons produced a number of books about the subject.

Domestic Practice of Hydropathy went into numerous editions. In it, Johnson laid out 74 therapies that would cure just about any condition that inflicted humankind, from constipation to consumption. Cures included repeatedly leaping in and out of shallow baths and plunge baths, alternate wet massage and dry massage, and a 'wash down with hot water, yellow soap and flannel'.

Dr Johnson also explained how the cure worked. 'I have shown that the pores of the skin joined end to end would form a tube 28 miles in length,' he wrote. 'Surely there can be no difficulty in believing that if this tube be obstructed and the matters which is intended to convey into the blood be kept out of it, surely I can say, there can be no difficulty in believing that a very unhealthy and wrong state of the blood must be the necessary result. How plain and common sense all this appears! How rational!'

CHAPTER THIRTEEN

All in the Mind

UST LIKE TODAY, MEDICS in old England had cures for the mind as well as the body – though some of them seem madder than the conditions they were trying to treat.

Imbecility

Anglo-Saxon books on leech craft said that imbecility could be cured by drinking lupins, fieldmore, bishopwort, cassia and alexander mixed with holy water and ale. *Leechdoms, Wortcunning and Starcraft of Early England* also recommends: 'Against a woman's chatter: taste at night fasting a root of radish, that day the chatter cannot harm thee.'

Lovesickness

In 1114 Thomas, Archbishop of York, was diagnosed with lovesickness. His doctors prescribed what was then the only known cure – a bout of therapeutic lovemaking. Thomas refused and died shortly afterwards. Since then other cures have been recommended – alcohol, catching the object of desire in an unflattering situation, beating and castration.

Madness

'In case a man be lunatic,' ran an old English cure from around 1100, 'take the skin of a mereswine' – literally a 'sea-swine', a dolphin or porpoise – 'work it into a whip. Swinge the man therewith, soon he will be well.'

Earlier, the Anglo-Saxons had taken a more compassionate approach. Pounded herbs and roots were to be mixed with ale and holy water, left overnight, then drunk the next day from a church bell. Hallucinations could be cured by eating wolf's flesh 'well sodden'. Walnuts were good for those with brain fatigue because of their sympathetic shape.

In the Isle of Skye, the cure was to lay the patient on an anvil. The blacksmith was then to raise his heaviest hammer and bring it down on the patient's forehead, pulling away at the last possible moment. The lunatic, it was thought, would be shocked back to sanity.

Work of the Devil

Many thought that insanity was visited on the unwary by the Devil. To protect against this, you could put lupins, worm-wood, bishopwort and other herbs into a big pot and put this under the altar while nine masses were being said. Then you added as much salt as you could find and sheep's grease, and brought it to the boil. The resulting goo was then smeared on the eyes of anyone expecting a nocturnal visit from the Dark Lord.

If all that was too much trouble, you could 'seek in the maw of young swallows for some little stones and mind that they touch neither earth nor water nor other stones'. When you had three of them, you placed them on the Devil's intended victim. However, chasing swallows around the fields and peering down their gullets might be considered a symptom of madness in itself.

In medieval times, it was thought that a cruise was good for lunacy, so lunatics were put on boats and sent out to sea – hence the term 'ship of fools'. It was, of course, a way of getting rid of them.

The Christian cure was to lash the lunatic to a cross for the night. This would scare the Devil out of them. Or you could haul lunatics off to one of the numerous shrines set up to cure them across Europe. You could sprinkle them with holy water, exorcise the Devil or, in severe cases, burn them.

Depression

In his classic *Anatomy of Melancholy*, the Anglican clergyman Robert Burton (1577–1640) states that the English are particularly susceptible to depression. It had something to do with the weather, the dampness or the food. But that did not mean it was incurable. He recommended that you take the head of a ram that had never 'meddled with a ewe', knock its horns off and boil the whole thing – 'skin and wool together' – until soft. The brains were then removed, sprinkled with herbs and cooked on hot coals. The patient was to live exclusively on a diet of this ram's brain for three days. When the three days were up, the patient would be noticeably happier.

Alternatively, the lungs of a ram could be applied hot to the forehead. A young lamb split along the spine would do. Again, the patient would be noticeably happier when the treatment was over.

Otherwise bezoars could be used. These are the calcified stones found in the gastrointestinal organs that were thought to have magical properties. A delicious drink made from bezoars, ambergrease, alkermes – the scarlet grain insect once

thought to be a berry – and water used to quench gold in bucked up the gloomy.

However, Burton had heard of another brew in the East that raised the spirits:

> The Turks have a drink called coffa (for they have no wine), so named of a berry as black as soot, and as bitter... which they sip still of, and sup as warm as they can suffer; they spend much time in those coffa-houses which are somewhat like our alehouses or taverns, and there they sit chatting and drinking to drive away the time, and to be merry together, because they find by experience that kind of drink, so used, helpeth digestion, and procureth alacrity. Some of them take opium to this purpose.

Twelve years after Burton died, the first coffee house opened in London. It was not until 1792 that William Tuke opened an asylum in York that used as its principal therapy afternoon tea.

Early psychotherapy

James Newton of Clerkenwell Green claimed to have a 'cure for melancholy, which is offered to distracted friends'. According to his handbill he also seemed to be able afford some miraculous cure to the insane:

> I'le name only three of the parish where I live. The first was a woman put to me by the churchwardens in 1672, who was very much given to swear and tear, having very grievous

sores made by binding her in bed with cords, yet she was perfectly cured in three weeks.

The second was a man void of sense and reason, who when his hands were at liberty, most vigorously beat himself and tore his hair off his head. He was perfectly cured in four days.

The third was a man put to me by the Overseers of the Poor in 1674, whose distemper varied from the other; wherefore, because I would not say he should be King Charles II, he commanded the standers-by to take off my head, for he would be King Charles whether I would or not. He was perfectly cured in six days.

Electric shock treatment

Lifelong incarceration in Bedlam or other mental hospitals was the alternative treatment, along with the regular diet of purges, vomits, beatings and dousing – as well as being put on display for the amusement of visitors. By 1760, however, the Methodist evangelist and part-time medico John Wesley was recommending electricity as 'the general and rarely failing remedy in nervous cases of every kind'. In 1796 Bedlam got its first electrical machine to add electric shocks to the other maltreatments it dished out. It was, however, not until the twentieth century that electro-convulsive therapy really came into its own.

Halting hysteria

According to Culpeper's *Complete Herbal*, the upward movement of the womb caused hysteria. The theory was that if the womb was denied the two things it craved – sex and babies – it would grow angry and start wandering around the body, fighting with other organs. It could, if sufficiently irate, reach the throat and strangle its host. To lure it down to its proper place, Culpeper said, smelly things such as asafoetida should be applied to the nose, while sweet perfumes such as civet were applied to the 'place of conception'. Once it was back in place, the belly should be bound to keep it there.

However, most doctors conceded that the best cure for an unhappy womb was the marriage bed. Writing in 1630, Nicholas Fonteyn said: 'Wives are more healthful than widows or virgins, because they are refreshed with the man's seed, and ejaculate their own, which, being excluded, the cause of evil' – the hysteria – 'is taken away.'

Maids's, nun's and widow's melancholy

Burton's *Anatomy of Melancholy* called hysteria 'maids's, nun's and widow's melancholy'. But if they had no husbands, how were the symptoms to be relieved? Simple. Physicians and midwives had long found that if they rubbed a woman's genitals until she experienced some sort of paroxysm, the hysteria would go. On no account were women to do this for themselves. After all, doctor knows best.

However, this was only a temporary cure. Women were prescribed horse riding, rope climbing and the use of rocking chairs. In some severe cases, it was recommended that pessaries made from certain irritants should be inserted into the vagina. This would heat the genitals and discharge any dangerous build-up of the woman's 'seed'.

Nineteenth-century surgeons took this much more seriously and whipped out a woman's ovaries at the first sign that she might have sexual needs. However, *The Family Medical Adviser* of 1852 was benign. 'Hysteria is a disease to which females are often subject,' it said. 'In the case of a sudden attack put the feet at once into warm water.'

CHAPTER FOURTEEN

Animal Magic

NIMALS HAVE PLAYED a significant part in the treatment of human disease. In ancient Greece, if you were licked by one of the dogs at the temple of Asclepius, the Greek god of healing, you would be restored to health. The first-century Roman writer Plutarch noted that if a jaundiced person stared at a stone-curlew, the bird stared back and 'draws out and receives the malady'. Bird sellers kept their cages covered to prevent people getting a free cure. To this day, in rural Jamaica there are some who think that if a large hairless dog is stretched out over a feverish patient it will draw the illness into itself. Sadly, animal cures may work for humans, but they do not often turn out well for the creatures concerned.

Toad power

In medieval times, to become a doctor you had to have a 'special power' and an old English collection of folk cures told you how to get it:

First get a toad. Take it to a graveyard and find a grave with an anthill on it. Bury the toad in the middle of the anthill, then return to the grave at midnight for the next three nights. On the fourth night, dig down into the anthill and you will find that the ants have eaten all the flesh of the toad, leaving only the bones. Take the bones and throw them into the stream. All the bones except one will float away downstream, which will go against the current. Get hold of this bone; it will give you special power.

Squirrels

The Anglo-Saxons were convinced of the healing properties of squirrels. Squirrel brain stewed in wine was used as a sedative. The lungs were bandaged over sore eyes and the ankle bone was carried around to ward off cramp.

Swallows

A remedy for dizziness from a book published in 1596 reads:

Take a young swallow from her nest when the crescent moon is in Virgo; cut off the head and let the blood run into a vessel containing white frankincense; stir thoroughly until the fluid thickens; then give it to the patient when the moon is waning, three days in succession... see to it that the patient does not became angry during the process of the cure.

Snails

Snails were the cure for just about everything. The juice extracted from a bucketful of snails covered with brown sugar and hung over a basin in a meat cloth overnight was used to cure sore throats. Drinking snail soup was a cure for the consumption; while a black snail rubbed nine times one way and nine times the other across a wart, then impaled on a black thorn, cured the affliction. In John Cohausen's 1743 medical directory *Hermippus Recidivus: Or, the Sage's Triumph Over Old Age and the Grave,* he recommends rubbing snail juice on your eyes to cure blindness.

Mice

In Victorian times, it was thought that letting mice run up and down the spine would cure a bad back.

Horse manure

In the late sixteenth century, a man named Peter Lelen was struck with debilitating pains in his sides. The doctor found that none of his normal cures worked, so he tried something new – beer with a dollop of horse dung in it. The physician noted that, from the patient's first sip, the concoction 'made all the blood in his veins boil, and put all his humours into such a general fermentation that he seemed to be in a boiling kettle'. Nevertheless, Lelen was cured, though ever afterwards he exhibited a craving for strong ale.

Pigeons

Pigeons were traditionally associated with death and it was thought that you could not die if you lay on pigeons' feathers. Samuel Pepys recorded that sick acquaintances of his surrounded themselves with pigeons. These included Catherine of Braganza, the wife of Charles II, who was very ill at the time.

Animals and epilepsy

In the sixteenth century the cure for epilepsy in children was eating 'the brain of a mountain goat drawn through a golden ring' or drinking 'the gall still warm from a dog who should have been killed at the moment the epileptic fell into the fit'. Epilepsy in children could be seen as a divine madness, but in young men it was a sure sign of masturbation or sexual excess. The cure was castration.

Rabbits

Animals could also be the symptom of a distressing condition. This was certainly the case with Mary Toft, who became famous as 'the women who gave birth to rabbits'.

The problem began in October 1726, when Mary, a mother of three in Godalming, Surrey, gave birth to what looked like pieces of cat. The midwife Mary Gill was so distressed that she called in John Howard, an experienced obstetrician from Guildford.

When he arrived, Mary's mother-in-law Ann Toft showed him several other body parts that she had delivered from Mary. They could have been from a pig or a cat, he said. The following day, Mary went into labour again. Howard delivered a rabbit and immediately felt another in her belly. By the time she had given birth to nine rabbits, Howard had moved her into his home in Guilford.

News of these miraculous events quickly spread. King George I became intrigued and sent the court anatomist Nathanael St André and a fellow of the Royal Society, Samuel Molyneux, to investigate. They, too, were quickly convinced and St André, who himself delivered five rabbits, wrote *A Short Narrative of an Extraordinary Delivery of Rabbits*, which became a bestseller.

Mary was then brought to London to be examined by Sir Richard Manningham, another fellow of the Royal Society and a leading obstetrician. He was more sceptical and had Mary confined to Lacy's Bagnio in Leicester Fields, where she could be kept under observation in a controlled setting. There leading surgeon James Douglas, who was also sceptical, examined her.

Under constant surveillance, the 'babies' which Mary had been producing daily stopped coming. Then, after a week, she went into labour. However, a porter at the bagnio named Thomas Howard told a justice of the peace that Mary had bribed him to bring the smallest rabbit she could find, and on 4 December 1726 Mary was arrested.

She eventually confessed, saying that her mother-in-law had put her up to it. Mary had simply taken animal parts, put them up her vagina and then discharged them. It had not seemed strange to Howard or any of her other supporters that none of her 'babies' had been born alive.

Mary was sent to the Bridewell, where she spent Christmas. But her imprisonment was an embarrassment to the authorities, particularly the king, who had taken her claims seriously, so she was released. She returned to Godalming where, in February 1727, she gave birth to daughter, a human one this time. She had been well and truly cured.

Bosom serpents

The Anglo-Saxons had the laughable belief that illness was caused by invisible elves that shot tiny arrows into the afflicted organ. By medieval times things had moved on and most internal illnesses were thought to be caused by 'bosom serpents' – snakes, worms, frogs, toads and lizards that took up residence in the parts of the body affected. Patients would regularly vomit up reptiles. The sure cure was a draft of horse's urine, which was guaranteed to flush them out. Or you could dangle a piece of bread on a hook and lower it down the patient's throat.

Ulcers and cancer were caused by worms and lice burrowing under the skin. The way to lure them out was to suspend the patient over a vat of warm water.

Worms

The idea that illness was caused by serpents and worms persisted and, in the eighteenth century, a powder know as *Pulvis Benedictus*, or Worm Exterminator, was advertised on pasteboards in London coffee houses. It was, the ad said, 'the only thing known, not only in England, but in the whole Europian World, of the kind'. As part of the pitch, the following stories were related: 'The first is of one Mr Stiles of the Lock and Key in West Smithfield, who was practically eaten by a worm eight feet long, and might still have been alive if he had only taken the Exterminator, which is looked upon to be rather a miracle than a medicine.'

In another, Mr Stubbs, a surgeon living at Stratton Ground

in Westminster, was 'about to embalm a Gentlewoman who had been dead eight and forty hours. When working at his operation, her heart leapt out upon the table, and out of it he took a worm as thick as an arrow, with two heads, one like a serpent.'

Unfortunately, the purveyor of this product, who lived at the Golden Ball in Devonshire Street outside Bishop's Gate, needed a 15-chapter book to explain the wonderful powers of this powder and the cures it effected – more than we have room for here. But he concluded by saying: 'Since it hath pleased Almighty God to send such medicines, I think it a great error in those that neglect them.'

CHAPTER FIFTEEN

Dodgy Dentistry

VEN TODAY, WHEN WE are blessed with anaesthetics, nobody likes going to the dentist, but while medical men had always sought palliative treatments and painless extractions, the results were usually excruciating.

Toothache cures

Since Roman times, it had been thought that toothache and tooth decay were caused by tooth worms that ate away the teeth. They first made their appearance in AD 41 in *De compositione medicamentorum* by Scribonis Largus, doctor to Messalina, the notoriously libidinous wife of the Emperor Claudius, but were still very much in play in old England.

In *Leechdoms, Wortcunning and Starcraft*, there were several cures:

> For tooth worms take acorn meal and henbane-seed and wax, of equally much. Mix them together. Make them into a wax candle and burn it. Let it reek into the mouth, put a black cloth under, then shall the worms fall on it.

For tooth wark [ache]: if a worm eat the tooth, take an old hollylead, hartwort and sage. Boil in water, pour it into a bowl and yawn over it; then the worms shall fall into the bowl.

For tooth wark, fray to dust the rind of a nut tree and thorntree; cut the teeth on the outside, shed the dust on frequently. For upper toothache take leaves of with, wind and wring them on the nose. For nether toothache, slit the gums with the instrument till they bleed.

Then comes the recipe for painless extraction:

Take some newts, by some called lizards, and those nasty beetles which are found in ferns in the summer time. Calcine them in an iron pot, and make a powder thereof, and apply to the tooth frequently, refraining from spitting it off; then the tooth will fall away without pain. It is proven.

Two centuries later, we get:

For aching of the hollow tooth: Take raven's dung and put it in the hollow tooth and colour it with the juice of pellitory-of-Spain [a plant similar to yarrow] that the sick recognise it not, nor know what it be; and then put it in the tooth and it shall break the tooth and take away the aching as some men say, it will make the tooth fall out.

Other cures for toothache get increasingly desperate. Laxatives, leeching, blistering of the skin, bloodletting, putting a clove of garlic in the ear, cupping and destroying the nerve by cauterising it with acid or a red-hot iron were all recommended, while medieval Frenchmen believed you could cure a toothache by spitting in the mouth of a frog.

Tooth-drawers

If none of the above worked, you would have to submit to the tooth-drawers, who performed at fairs or in bazaars or market-places. Their sign was a banner and a parasol with a small piece of alligator hanging from it. This signified the small 'alligator tail' stuffed into the empty socket to staunch the bleeding. The 'alligator' here probably derives from the old English verb 'alligate', meaning to tie up or bind. Tooth-drawers also wore a necklace of human teeth and a pointed hat bearing the insignia of St Apollonia, patron saint of toothache. Born in Alexandria, Apollonia refused to renounce Christ during the persecutions of 249 AD and had all her teeth broken and extracted, a common Roman torture. To escape any further oral attention, she jumped into a fire and was burnt to death. Even though Apollonia's teeth had been smashed, it seems that they were not hard to come by in the Middle Ages. When Henry VI tried to stamp out the trade in religious relics, he ordered anyone possessing relics to hand them over to his agents. The seventeenth-century church historian Thomas Fuller said: 'A ton of veritable teeth of St Apollonia were thus

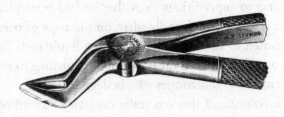

collected together, and were her stomach proportionate to her teeth, a country could scarce afford her a meal.'

Tooth drawing was a popular public entertainment, often accompanied by clowns, jugglers and conjurers. The noise of the crowd they drew covered the patient's screams. From old paintings we can deduce that the patient also stood a good chance of having his pockets picked while the tooth-drawer was at work.

J. Menzies Campbell described the activities of itinerant tooth-drawers in seventeenth-century Scotland:

> A horde of arrogant mountebanks whose policy was never that of self-abnegation, systematically travelled around the country, their visits coinciding with local markets and fairs... They glibly promised cures for every disease including toothache. There was a zany who, in a droll manner, sang lewd yet amusing songs riveting the attention of disorders which his master could cure.

The entourage also included dancers with curious antics and performers on the tight rope. The bedizened quicksilver enlivened the proceedings with comic orations, while perched on a well-appointed chariot drawn by four (sometimes six) elegantly caparisoned horses. Not infrequently, he reinforced his claims by quoting scripture or by prayers to saints. Although never averse to superstitious cases that he had miraculously cured, he remained profoundly silent on the array of persons he had caused to suffer grievously or even liquidated. Tooth drawing was always one of the most popular sidelines to entertain the crowd of ignoramuses who besieged his stage.

However, none of this was really necessary. According to

Scottish folk medicine toothache could be prevented by carrying around a sheep's tooth or a mole's paw, a cure still recommended by John Wesley centuries later. In Wales, chewing snake skins marinated in vinegar was considered the cure, while generally it was found that throwing henbane on the fire was enough to take the pain away. This contains a powerful cocktail of dangerous narcotics, which could be inhaled.

Royal extractions

Even monarchs had to subject themselves to the not-so-gentle art of the tooth-drawer. Elizabeth I, particularly, suffered from pyorrhoea. A German visitor to her court in 1598 reported 'her lips are narrow and her teeth black, a defect that the English seem subject to, from their great use of sugar'. And she was a martyr to toothache. In his *Life of Bishop Aylmer*, the ecclesiastic historian John Strype relates:

It was in the month of December 1578, when she [the Queen] was so excessively tormented with the Distemper [toothache] that she had no intermission day or night, and it forced her to pass whole nights without taking any rest; and it came to that extremity, that her physicians were called in and consulted…

The pulling it out was esteemed the safest way; to which, however, the Queen, as was said, was very averse, as afraid of the acute pain that accompanied it. And now it seems it was that the Bishop of London being present, a man of high courage, persuaded her that the pain was not so much, and not at all to be dreaded; and to convince her thereof told her, she should have a sensible experience of it in himself, though he were an old man, and had not many teeth to spare; and immediately had the surgeon come and pull out one of his teeth, perhaps a decayed one, in her Majestie's Presence. Which accordingly was done: and She was hereby encouraged to submit to the operation herself.

Eventually all of Elizabeth's teeth fell out, and by 1602, when she appeared in public, she 'putteth fine cloths in her mouth to bear out her checks'.

George III, however, was much more sanguine. Once when he was about to have one of his teeth extracted, he asked his dentist for a glass of brandy. When it was proffered, he declined. 'I have no need of it,' he said, 'but was merely anxious to observe if your hand was steady.'

Teething

In times when the bones of saints were widely available, they were popular as teething rings. The bones of St Hugh were particularly effective. The story goes that St Hugh was a great lover of children and when they were having teething troubles he dipped his finger in holy water and passed it gently over their gums nine times. When he removed his finger the last time, out popped the tooth.

If seems that even the bones of a bogus St Hugh would do. A young woman had been married for a long time to an elderly knight. They had no children and she asked her confessor what she could do about it. Later he approached her while she was sitting alone in a garden, representing himself as St Hugh. He would, he said, make up for her lack of children that evening in the chapel after vespers – and did so in the normal fashion.

After the baby was born, it had trouble teething and grew dangerously ill. The bogus St Hugh was already dead, but the lady dreamt that, if she got one of the saint's toes and rubbed the child's gum with it, it would be well again. She bribed the sexton, and the coffin was opened and a toe removed. She then rubbed the bone on the child's gum. Immediately two teeth came through and the child recovered.

Necklaces

Major John Choke, of 'Elixir for the Morow-Cure' fame (see page 59), also came up with 'most famous and in a manner Miraculous Necklaces for easing children in breeding teeth and cutting them without pain'. He said:

> The best time to put them on is when they are two months old and two wear them until they have bred all their teeth, and none are troubled with the Evil or Falling sickness [epilepsy]… The names of the parents of children that have made use of the Virtuous Necklaces are the Countess of Northumberland, Lady Bartees at St James's, Lord Burleys, Sir William Drake in Bucks, Sir Edward Turner in Essex, Mrs Grooms in Windmill-street near Pickadilly, Mrs Flowers in Pye-alley in Fan-church street and others.

Anodyne Necklaces, as they became called in the eighteenth century, were sold by Mr Burchell of Long Acre, who said they were invented by Dr Tanner and recommended by 'Dr Paul Chamberlen', the scion of a long line of male midwives. Burchell proclaimed:

> Virtues of the same being so large, I thought fit as in duty and was bound to my fellow Christians to revive this worthy Anodyne from the ashes which hath been advantageous to all mankind. Being not much bigger in weight than a nut-meg, absolutely easeth all children in breeding and cutting of teeth without pain; and also children that have so worn them, have been stronger at nine months than them of twelve.

The beads of these necklaces seem to have been made of peony wood, which was recommended by Orbasius, a fifth-century Roman physician, for the prevention of epilepsy.

Oral hygiene

The English Man's Treasure of 1613 warned lovers that foul breath would put off the opposite sex and it was recommended: 'To take away the stinking of the mouth – wash mouthe with water and vinegar and chew masticke then wash moute with the decoction of annis seeds, mints and cloves sodden in wine.'

In earlier times, it was said that you could guard against bad breath by gargling with your own urine in the morning.

Whiter than white

In seventeenth-century England, there were no toothbrushes for home use – or bathrooms to put them in, for that matter – and teeth cleaning was left in the hands of professional barber-surgeons. For a truly dazzling smile, they would scrape the teeth, and then swab them with *aqua fortis*. This 'strong water'

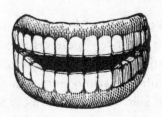

was actually nitric acid. While this left the teeth whiter than white to start with, repeated applications ate away the enamel, destroying the tooth.

Dentists

To this day, the English are mocked for their bad teeth, but things were a lot worse before the mid-seventeenth century when the art of dentistry came over from France. At first practitioners were known as 'operators for teeth' and apprenticed themselves to barbers, where they scraped and swabbed teeth and worked with ivory and gold to make false ones.

Peter de la Roche seems to have been the first practitioner in London. He was appointed 'Operator to the King's teeth'. On 11 March 1661, Samuel Pepys records in his diary: 'At night home and found my wife come home, and she had got her teeth done new by la Roche, and are indeed now pretty and handsome, and I was much pleased with it.'

At first these operators did not move into the territory of the tooth-drawers. Instead they specialised in cleaning teeth. Later, cleaning powders were being sold for home use. The *Daily Courant* in 1717 carried an advertisement for a powder that read:

It at once makes the teeth white as ivory, tho' never so black or yellow, and effectively preserves them from rotting or decaying, continuing them sound to exceeding old age. It wonderfully cures the scurvy in the gums, prevents rheum or defluxions, kills worms at the roots of the teeth, and thereby hinders the toothache. It admirably fastens loose teeth, being neat and cleanly medicine of a pleasant and graceful scent.

Extractions

Operators for teeth began to take over from tooth-drawers and started to extract teeth when a new instrument called a dental key, or just plain key, was introduced in 1725. It had a claw on one end to grip the tooth and a handle like the grip of a simple corkscrew on the other. The claw was hooked over the crown, and then the handle was twisted, ripping the tooth from its socket. The English called it the German key, while the Germans and French called it the English key.

It was only in the 1750s that the word dentist – from the French *dentiste* – came into the English language. Many were largely self-taught. As late as 1840, it was noted that to set up as a dentist 'a brass plate and brazen effrontery [were] all the diplomas necessary'.

Even those taken on as apprentices did not get much training before they set about torturing patients of their own. One trainee noted:

The mode of instructing me that Mr Sheffield adopted was to work with me at the bench and occasionally to take me into his surgery, where I saw him operate. I was also at his side when he saw the gratis patients who came to him each morning at nine o'clock to be relieved of pain. I did all the mechanical working during my apprenticeship, and after about three months he gave the care of his gratis patients into my hands, and I well remember when I went down alone to extract my first tooth, which I am happy to say I accomplished successfully.

An Act of Parliament requiring all dentists in Britain to be fully qualified was only introduced in 1878. Until then they had been trained privately and practised without a licence.

Van Butchell

One of the most popular dentists of the 1770s was the bearded Martin van Butchell, who made 'real or artificial teeth from one to an entire set, with superlative gold pivots and springs: also gums, sockets and palate, formed, fitted, finished and fixed, without drawing stumps or causing pain'. He rode about London on a white pony that had purple spots painted on it and kept his dead wife embalmed in a glass case in his surgery. However, when he married again, his new wife insisted that the dear departed move out.

Scientific advances

The first book on dentistry written in English was *Disorders of the Teeth and Gums*. It appeared in 1768 and was written by Thomas Berdmore, dentist to King George III. He noted that the patent powder available at that time would wear away a tooth's enamel with just four hours brushing. On the other hand, not brushing caused the build-up of tartar.

The scientific study of dentistry began with the great surgeon John Hunter in the 1770s. He recommended whipping out decayed teeth, boiling them and sticking them back into the socket again. Otherwise he would burn away the nerve of the affected tooth with sulphuric or nitric acid. He also believed in fighting fire with fire. One cure for the toothache he recommended was burning the patient's ear with hot irons.

Knock-out cure

In 1799 the chemist Sir Humphrey Davy, relentless experimenter and inventor of the miner's safety lamp, began using nitrous oxide – also known as laughing gas – as an anaesthetic to ease the pain of toothache, after first testing it on himself. Later he almost killed himself inhaling 'water gas' – a mixture of carbon monoxide and hydrogen sometimes used as a fuel. However, it was only in 1844 that two Americans – the inventor Gardner Colton and the dentist Horace Wells – mixed nitrous oxide with oxygen, and this was administered to Wells while his assistant took out one of his teeth. Wells's student, the dentist William Morgan, then developed ether.

Old remedies for toothache

In the nineteenth century, some of the old folk cures still survived. For toothache, a *Book for Every Home* recommended putting a little scraped horseradish around the root, while an *Old Corner Cupboard* prescribed one teaspoon each of ground ginger and Epsom salts, taken in a teacup of hot water.

To prevent toothache in the first place, John Wesley recommended that you 'rub the teeth often with tobacco ashes', or 'lay roast parings of turnips, as hot as may be, behind the ear', or 'wear around the neck a double hazelnut – this not only cures the complaint, but you will never suffer from the pain again'. And teeth could be cleaned with a pinch of soot from the chimney.

However, the *Wensleydale Advertiser* of 1844 took a more brutal view. There are 'two certain cures for toothache,' it said, 'either pulling out or driving further in'. By then, the teeth from the 50,000 corpses left on the battlefield after Waterloo had been harvested . These were used to make dentures and as transplants that were known at 'Waterloo teeth'.

CHAPTER SIXTEEN

Strange Surgery

EFORE ANAESTHETICS surgery was a brutal business. It was also more debilitating, if you needed a limb amputating; embarrassing, if something had gone wrong below the waist; and more life-threatening, especially before the development of antiseptics.

Ano, domini!

The most important English surgeon of the medieval period was John of Arderne (1306–90). After seeing service in France during the Hundred Years' War, he practised for the last 20 years of his life in Newark in Nottinghamshire. His specialisation was disease of the rectum and he is sometimes referred to as the father of proctology.

Ironically, like many modern doctors, he made patients pay through the nose. He wrote: '…for the cure of fistula in ano, when it is curable, ask he competently, of a worthy man and a great, an hundred marks or forty pound, with robes and fees of an hundred shilling term of like by year'. That is, he charged a rich patient a hundred shillings (£1,000 in today's money) for every year he lived after the operation. 'Of lesser men forty pound or forty marks ask he without fees; and take he naught less than an hundred shillings. For never in my life took I less than an hundred shillings for cure of sickness.'

The best known of Arderne's manuscripts, written in 1376, concerned the treatment of anal fistula, which had previously been considered incurable. Arderne would bend his patient over, then thread a ligature through the fistula's opening into the rectum. Then he incised the outer wall of the fistula and laid open the entire tract. There was often more than one patient to be dealt with and he would work his way around them, using sponges to staunch the blood. The pain can only be imagined. However, much the same procedure is used today, although we now have anaesthetics.

Then there are abscesses: '…an abscess breeding near the anus should not be left to burst by itself,' he wrote, 'but the surgeon should busily feel with his finger the place of the abscess, and where so is found any softness, there, the patient not knowing, carefully, be it boldly opened with a very sharp lancette…'

Rectal cancer he called an 'owl boil' as owls liked to hide in dark places. He treated it with enemas of bran porridge. An operation was out of the question.

He was not a great one for salves, although he would occasionally apply a mixture of fine flour and egg white to wounds. His methods were not always successful. In fact, his cures may well have contributed to the deaths of his patients. He recorded one such instance:

A gardener who worked with vines cut his hand on the Friday after Saint Thomas of Canterbury's Day. His thumb was cut nearly off, and could be folded up next to the underarm, bleeding profusely. The treatment was as follows. First the thumb was put back in place and sewn on. The bleeding was then curtailed with Lanfranc's red powder and hare bristles…

It is now known that hair from a hare is often crawling with tetanus bacilli, which may well explain the outcome in this case.

…On the third day, the bandage was removed, and the bleeding had stopped. Then medicaments were applied which bring forth blood, and we changed the bandage daily. The wound began to clean itself, and the pus came out. But on the fourth, blood emerged at around midnight, and the patient lost nearly two pounds. The bleeding was stopped and a new bandage applied. On the eleventh day, even more

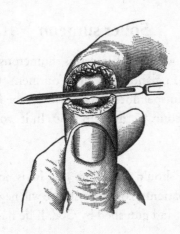

blood emerged than the first time. We stopped it again, but in the morning, the patient suffered bad cramps in the jaws and arm, unable to feed himself or open his mouth. On the fifteenth day, he bled uncontrollably. The cramps continued and, on the twentieth day, he died.

The incubation time and the lockjaw indicated that the patient died of tetanus. It is not known what Lanfranc's red powder was. The red powder may have been pimpinella, the plant that produces aniseed seeds and the spice anise. According to the Swedish author Advidh Månsson's *A Very Useful Herb-book*: 'Pimpinella draws out iron and thorns easily from wounds with no pain, if one lays a little leaf around the wound; thus in Latin it is called *Sanguisorba*, meaning blood-sucker or blood-drinker.'

Another theory is that it was peony, whose seeds have been used to treat tetanus since Roman times. Peony, as we have seen, was also a Roman cure for the falling-sickness.

Sober surgeon

Along with the works of Paracelsus, numerous medical text-books came to England from the Continent. One such was Heinrich von Pfolspeundt's *Bündt-Ertzney*, the first treatise on surgery published in German, in 1460. In it, von Pfolspeundt wrote:

The surgeon should make sure that he is not drunk when treating his patients. For otherwise he will neglect them, and will be guilty and punished by God. If he has eaten onions or beans, or spent the previous night with an impure lady, he should be careful not to breathe on any wounds.

He also recommended that the surgeon wash his hands.

By 1565 things had moved on a bit. In his 'most excellent and learned woorke of chirurgerie', called *Chirurgia parua Lanfranci*, the Maidstone surgeon John Halle said: 'A surgeon should not be mis-created, deformed, goggle or squint-eye, unhealthy of body, imperfect of mind, not whole in his members, nor boisterous of fingers, or having shaking hands.'

Barber-surgeons

Henry VIII sought to regulate the practice of medicine, which proved rather problematic. In 1511 there had been a dispute between the Company of Barbers and the Guild of Surgeons about who should regulate surgery in London. Henry put an end to it by placing the capital's medical profession under the control of the Bishop of London, who issued licences allowing physicians and surgeons to practise. In 1530 new rules for barbers and surgeons were agreed by the Lord Chancellor, Sir Thomas More. This document is still held by the Worshipful Company of Barbers at Barber-Surgeons' Hall and its writ ran within a radius of one mile from the Cities of London and Westminster.

Ten years later the Guild of Surgeons and the Company of Barbers were amalgamated by Act of Parliament, which, among other privileges, granted the united company the bodies of four executed criminals for dissection each year. But

Henry well knew the difference between a barber and a surgeon. The Annals of the Barber-Surgeon's Company record that the chief of the king's barbers was ordered to be present for the court's Saturday bath, whenever 'it pleased the King to wash his head, legs and feet'. However, members of the guild were forbidden 'to shave, wash the beard, or polish anyone's teeth on a Sunday'. Other rules forbade any apprentice in surgery to wear a beard, which meant anything that 'has grown more than 15 days'.

The barbers and surgeons stuck it out until the eighteenth century. Then came the parting of the ways. By 1745 the surgeons outnumbered barbers in the city. They petitioned the House of Commons, and the bill making the surgeons and barbers of London two separate and distinct companies received the royal assent on 2 May 1745. However, old-fashion barbers still commemorate the link between the two professions with the red-and-white barbers' pole. This is

supposed to symbolise the bandage wrapped around the arm during bloodletting.

Like a hole in the head

In old England trepanning was commonplace. Archaeological evidence shows that it was carried out since prehistoric times. A hole about an inch in diameter was cut in the skull. It is thought that this let evil spirits out of the brain, or let the sunlight in. Amazingly, in ancient times most people survived this procedure. Often in was carried out more than once. An Inca skull found in Cuzco, Peru, had seven boreholes in it.

Prince Rupert, a Royalist commander in the English Civil War, was trepanned twice in 1667. At that time Prince Rupert was a privy councillor in the Restoration government and a commander in the Navy. He went on to become the first governor of the Hudson's Bay Company in 1670 and to fight in the Third Dutch War of 1672–4. He died in London in 1682, fifteen years after two inch-wide holes had been cut in his head. Trepanning continued into modern times in Melanesia and rural Algeria. Currently the procedure is still performed in hospital to relieve the pressure caused by a build-up of blood in the cranium following a severe head injury.

Illustrated surgery

In the seventeenth century surgeons, like physicians, published handbills detailing the services they offered. In 1670 the 'Professor of Physick and Oculist' John Russell, who lived at the 'Two Blew Posts against Gray's Inn in Holbourn', issued an illustrated bill showing the operations he specialised in.

It showed him at work on a rupture, trepanning a man whose skull had been fractured, tapping a patient suffering from dropsy, cutting off a large wen, operating on a hairlip, sewing up a fistula, extracting a nasal polyp, operating on a breast, couching a cataract, performing other operations on the eye and removing the stem of a tobacco pipe that had been lodged in a man's mouth, the captions says, for three days.

For God's sake

John Newman, 'a most expert chyrurgian', operated on a stage on Moorfields, a popular showcase for medical men of the seventeenth century.

> I shall not trouble your ears to give you an account of the operations I have performed in many parts of England and other places beyond the seas but shall only mention what operations I have perform'd on my stage since March 28, 1679, when I cut a large wen the bigness of a penny loaf from off the throat of Robert Bond, a carman, and is now very well. On April 2, I cut a large rupture from Michael Butts … I cure the poor of wens and hair lips, for God's sake.

Caesareans

Birth by Caesarean section was always a risky practice. It is said that when Jane Seymour, Henry VIII's third wife, was nearing her time in 1537, Henry told his doctors that the child should be saved at all costs. After all, as he had already amply demonstrated, it was easy enough to find a new wife. As it was, the future Edward VI survived and Jane Seymour died soon after. In fact, Jane was already ill and a Caesarean in such a case would have been justified even today. Henry really loved Jane and the story may have been put about to discredit him.

The name Caesarean comes from Caesar, as Julius Caesar is said to have been born that way. There is no evidence for this. Indeed, Julius Caesar's mother, Aurelia, was still alive when he invaded Britain, so the operation was certainly not carried out post-mortem. Another story is that the name derived from a law passed in Rome in 715 BC, which prohibited a woman who had died during pregnancy being buried until the foetus was surgically removed. The two bodies were then disposed of separately – although the Romans usually cremated their dead rather than bury them. When Julius Caesar came to power, he ordered the codifying of Roman law and this old law became part of the Lex Caesare. As it dictated the removal of the – in some cases living – foetus from the dead mother, the birth by section became 'Caesarean'.

There is an obvious danger in slicing people open. Paracelsus believed that, just as an egg goes off if the shell is cracked or an apple rots if the skin is breached, air causes damage to the human body if it reaches the tissue under the skin. Consequently, in 1784, the Edinburgh obstetrician John Aitkin began performing Caesareans with the patient in a bathtub. That way the water would keep the air out of the abdominal cavity once the incision was made.

The following year, a Dr Cowley described in the *London Medical Journal* how he had seen a 'negress' cut open her own belly with a long sharp knife and pull out a child. She was then sewn up by a vet and, apparently, survived.

Unfortunately the mother did not survive in a most extraordinary accidental Caesarean quoted by Swedish medical writer Knut Haeger in *The Illustrated History of Surgery*. Apparently a soldier's pregnant wife was fetching water from a river when she was hit by a cannon ball, which literally split her in two. The baby popped out and fell in the water. The child was rescued by some troopers and lived.

The scourge of stones

Gentlemen, particularly, wanted to avoid stones forming in the bladder. These could be remedied by inserting a rod up the tract of the penis, which dislodged them if they were obstructing the urethra.

If they could not be moved this way and the blockage continued, the build-up of urine in the bladder became so painful that the patient would consent to undergo the almost unimaginably excruciating experience of lithotomy. After the patient assumed the position women adopt for a gynaecological examination, the surgeon would slice open the perineum that runs between the anus and the scrotal sack. The urine would then be drained. A finger would be inserted up the patient's anus to push the stone forwards and, if the stonecutter was deft enough, the stones were removed. All this was done without an anaesthetic, and with no antiseptics, there was a distinct possibility that you would die.

Attempts were regularly made to treat stones without surgery. The prominent physician Richard Lower (1631–91) came up with this formulation:

> To alleviate a stone-attack and the usually consequent retention of urine, take snail shells and bees in equal quantities, dry them in a moderately hot oven, and grind them to a very fine powder. Take as much of this as a sixpence holds, dissolve it in a quarter mug of bone-meal water, and give it on an empty stomach, followed by two hours of fasting, every day for three days in a row. It has often been found to break down the stone and drive the urine forth.

There were other patent medicines to save a seventeenth-century gentleman from the stonecutter. One stone-solvent in London was a German doctor who lived in Petty-France, Westminster. He claimed that his powder 'which with the blessing of God upon it certainly cures the stone and saveth those that have been designed to be cut for it. It wonderfully dissolves great stones and brings them away.'

These concoctions did not seem to work for Judge Jeffreys, who handed down 331 death sentences and sold hundreds into slavery in the colonies at the 'Bloody Assizes' after the failure of the Monmouth Rebellion of 1685. He galloped through cases at breakneck speed, allowing no time for a defence. This was because he suffered from bladder stones, which made urinating painful and meant that he had to go to the lavatory almost hourly.

Famous sufferers

The diarist Samuel Pepys was also a sufferer. At the age of 22 he had a stone the size of a tennis ball removed by leading lithotomist Thomas Hollister of Bart's. The operation was performed in the home of Mrs Turner, as the well-off avoided hospitals, which were dirty, disease-ridden and offered no aftercare. Only the poor suffered those conditions.

The operation was a success, although Pepys continued to suffer from the complaint and often passed 'gravel in his urine'. He never had children and it has been assumed that the perineal incision rendered him sterile – a frequent complication. It did not stop him having a vigorous sex life, though, as his diaries attest. Indeed, it is thought that irritation caused by scar tissue in such a sensitive area made Pepys so priapic.

To stave off more stones, Pepys drank turpentine. This was not a good idea as it causes damage to the kidneys. In fact, Pepys died of chronic inflammation of the kidneys and urinary poisoning. He also carried a hare's foot. When this provided little relief, a friend pointed out that it would only work if the foot included a joint.

Other famous sufferers include Oliver Cromwell, Isaac Newton, Francis Bacon, George VI, Robert and Horace Walpole, Peter the Great of Russia, Leopold I of Belgium and Napoleon III of France. One self-interested sufferer was Thomas Sydenham (1624–89), the pioneer of internal medicine. He said in despair of the condition: 'The patient suffers until he is finally consumed by both age and illness, and the poor man is happy to die.'

Salvation from the stonecutter

Eighteenth-century gentlemen were understandably terrified of the stonecutter, so when a young woman named Joanna Stephens claimed in 1738 to be able to cure kidney and bladder stones without recourse to the knife everyone wanted to hear what she had to say. Her potions convinced some of the major physicians and scientists of the day and she agreed to reveal the recipe for her remedy to the British public for a mere £5,000 (£311,000 in today's money). A fund for wealthy men to contribute to was launched. Even the Prime Minister Robert Walpole, himself a sufferer, subscribed. However, only £1,365 was raised (£85,030 today) and it appeared that this vital cure might be lost to the nation.

Parliament therefore set up a commission, including the most eminent medical men of the day, to look into the matter. They proclaimed that Joanna's remedy was the real thing and the British government handed over the rest of the money. They got their money's worth. Joanna then revealed that she had no less than three medicines for the condition. One was a concoction of honey, herbs and soap. A second contained snails and eggshell. A third was a pill made of burdock, snails, carrots and other commonplace ingredients, all put in a pot and charred until they were black.

Joanna disappeared with her £5,000, but there was no hue and cry. Gentlemen continued taking her potions for some considerable time to come as, even though they were ineffective, they were preferable to going under the knife. Prime Minister Robert Walpole was so afraid of the stonecutter that he underwent the soap cure. This consisted of consuming one ounce of alicant soap in three parts of limewater a day. He continued this for years and, by the time of his death, it is estimated that he had consumed 180 pounds of soap and 1,200 gallons of limewater. When he died in 1745, the post-mortem found three large stones in his bladder and it is even thought the treatment killed him.

'Sir Robert was killed by a lithontriptic medicine,' said his son, the writer Horace Walpole. He claimed that his father was not the only one to fall foul of the doctors of the time, 'Lord Bolingbroke by a man who pretended to cure him of a cancer in his face, and Winnington was physicked and bled to death by a quack in a few days for a slight rheumatism.'

Liston

In the days before anaesthetics, a surgeon needed to be quick to minimise the pain and trauma of an operation. Robert Liston (1794–1847), professor of clinical surgery at University College London, was known for his speed and dexterity. He removed a 45-pound scrotal tumour in four minutes flat and boasted of the speed that he could amputate a limb, shouting

'Time me, gentlemen, time me' to the students watching in the galleries above.

In one famous case, he amputated a leg in two and a half minutes, but in his enthusiasm he cut off the patient's testicles as well. However, Liston appears to have been slow compared to Napoleon's private surgeon Baron Dominique Larreu, who claimed to have amputated a man's leg in 14 seconds.

In another speedy amputation, Liston cut off the fingers of his young assistant and slashed the coat-tails of a distinguished surgeon who was observing. The patient died afterwards on the ward – a common occurrence in the days before Joseph Lister introduced antiseptics. The assistant died of gangrene and the surgical spectator died of fright at the sight of the flashing blade. This is said to be the only operation in history to claim 300 per cent mortality.

Although Sir Humphry Davy had discovered the anaesthetic properties of nitrous oxide nearly 50 years before, it was a couple of American dentists who developed laughing gas and ether for surgical use. On 21 December 1846, Robert Liston performed the first operation under anaesthesia in England. The amputated leg hit the sawdust after two and a half minutes as usual, but the need for speed in surgery was now outdated. When the patient, a butler named Frederick Churchill, awoke on the operating table, he raised himself up and

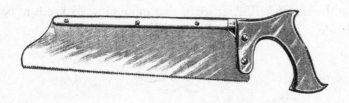

said: 'When are you going to begin? Take me back, I can't have it done.' He was then shown the stump, and wept.

Next to Godliness surgery

Cleanliness in hospitals might not seem such a curious cure now, but it certainly was considered so when Florence Nightingale went into nursing in 1853. She found hospital wards with 60 people crammed into one room, whose windows were covered with fungus and slime, as they were not opened for months on end to conserve heat. Sheets were not changed between patients and mattresses were never changed. The floors were covered with dried blood and other waste matter. Patients were in danger from infection simply from living in such conditions.

Joseph Lister pioneered the use of carbolic acid to kill germs in 1865. He went on to use antiseptic sprays and sterilised instruments to prevent infection, although surgeons still operated with their bare hands and in their everyday clothes. Gloves were introduced in 1878, when surgeon William Halsted's fiancée and surgical assistant found that the bichloride solution used to sterilise instruments caused eczema on her hands.

In 1897 the mess in the wards was finally cleared up when trained nurses were employed in all British hospitals. However, in the age of MRSA, it seems that more progress needs to be made.

Non-intervention

Caution should be exercised when it comes to surgery, as Peter Lowe pointed out in his book *The Whole Art of Chyrurgery*, published in London in 1612. Lowe was the personal physician to James VI of Scotland – James I of England – and had spent 30 years as a surgeon on the battlefields of Europe. He wrote:

> I remember from Paris in 1590, when a famous captain (my good friend Jayle, one of the highest chiefs in the Spanish Regiment) suffered an aneurysm [an abnormal swelling of a blood vessel]. As the oldest surgeon in the regiment, I was sent for, and I found it to be an aneurysm which should not be disturbed. My good friend Andrew Scot, who at the time has a large practice in Paris and was very clever at surgery, considered the same. We prescribed remedies against its growth, and sent to the apothecary. But he had already told the Captain that he did not believe in medicines for apostumet, as he called it, so he sent for a barber who was as ignorant as himself. The barber swore that he had instruments and other measures for every illness. Thus without further ado, he opened the swelling with a lancet, and blood spewed out so violently that the Captain died some hours later. I do not doubt that many such mistakes of the art are committed by fools in these countries.

CHAPTER SEVENTEEN

Odd Oculists

N OLD ENGLAND there were numerous causes of blindness and, in the days before anaesthetics, there can have been few more unpleasant things than to have doctors sticking needles and lancets in your eyes.

Royal oculist

The British royal family first used an eye doctor in the seventeenth century, when Thomas Clarck became official oculist to Charles II and his brother, who became James II, 'in whose presence he couched a cataract in a lady 15 years blind and restored her sight in an instant'. Couching was done by sticking a needle in the eye to push the opaque lens out of the line of vision.

In his handbills, Clarck also claimed to have treated a patient who was attacked by a burglar who knocked him down 'with a piece of iron, then battered and flatted his face, and twisted his hands in his hair, placed his thumbs in the corner of both his eyes and by a violence forced them out. In this barbarous manner he was brought to me: yet with God's assistance I replaced the eyes and restored him to perfect sight again.'

Oculist-in-ordinary

Queen Anne's oculist Sir William Read not only tended to her 'weak eyes', but also his advertisement claimed that he had 'cured the poor of blindness, cancers, wens, hair lips, wry necks and deafness for charity'.

Read was originally a tailor from Aberdeen, but had been practising as an all-round medical practitioner for some time.

When Read came to London and opened a practice in York Buildings in the Strand, his advertising came to the attention of Queen Anne, who appointed him oculist-in-ordinary. In 1707 he was knighted 'as a mark of Royal favour for his great services done in curing great numbers of seamen and soldiers of blindness, gratis'. Britain was involved in the War of the Spanish Succession on the Continent at the time, as well as fighting the French in India and North America.

Read's favoured cure for problems with the sight was putting 'the juice of goose dung or the white part of hen's dung into the eye'. He did not approve of the old remedies of 'licking the eye with the tongue or smoothing it with a gold ring'.

Nor did he agree with the popular cure for weak eyes, which was to 'drink a large draft of beer every morning', saying, 'I am persuaded that thousands have drunk themselves blind by this practise'.

After the death of Queen Anne Read became sworn oculist-in-ordinary to George I in 1714, but died in Rochester the following year.

Roger Grant took Read's position at court. He had begun life as a tinker and then became an Anabaptist preacher, before specialising in eyes. George I seems to have been very satisfied with him, though – but then George I employed a royal surgeon who also worked in the dispensary at Westminster Hospital. He was a dancing master, a fencing master and an accomplished linguist, but sadly he had no medical qualifications whatsoever.

Ophthalmiator pontificial

After Roger Grant, three generations of the same family were eye doctors to royals from the reign of George II to that of George VI. The line began with John Taylor, who styled himself 'Chevalier' and claimed to be 'Ophthalmiator Pontificial, Imperial and Royal, who treated Pope Benedict XIV, Augustus

III, King of Poland, Frederick V, King of Denmark and Norway, and Frederick Adolphus, King of Sweden'. An accomplished womaniser, he also claimed to have visited every convent in Europe – in pursuance of his profession, of course. Because of Grant's inflated sense of his own importance, many accused him of being a quack, but a medical observer watched him couching a cataract and was impressed. 'Taylor makes a small puncture with the lancet through the coat of the eye in the ordinary place of piercing with a needle in this operation,' he said. After checking to see if the cataract will separate, he 'introduces his needle and ruptures the cataract along its lower edge then pushes his needle down into the vitreous humour of eye'. Then he 'thrusts the altered crystalline out of the aperture already made in the lower parts of its capsule', and finally 'brings his needle back and pushes the cataract into the divided part of the vitreous humour'.

This technique had only been perfected in France some ten years before and is, roughly speaking, how cataract operations are done today – only then they were done without anaesthetic.

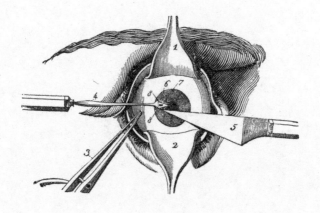

On the other hand, Taylor claimed to have discovered the secret of perpetual motion and to have cured Johann Sebastian Bach of his blindness at the age of 88 – although Bach died blind at 65. He also wrote the book *The Art of Making Love with Success*, which was published in Italy. Sadly, all copies of it seem to have been lost.

George III employed Taylor's son John Taylor II as his oculist, then his grandson John Taylor III, who went on to become oculist to George VI.

The first contact lens

The royal astronomer Sir John Herschel came up with the idea of the contact lens in 1827. Contact lenses were manufactured by German physiologist Adolf Fick 60 years later, in 1887.

CHAPTER EIGHTEEN

The Beauty Business

S A SIDELINE, DOCTORS have always developed beauty products or other aids to make their patients more sexually attractive. It was a lucrative business.

The beauty business first

After the Puritans fell from power and Charles II was restored to the throne, the demand for beauty products boomed. Beauty specialists established their business in the area around Mayfair. One particularly well-educated lady doctor set up shop in Bond Street. For 40 years she claimed to have been studying all manner of 'physick, chymical, gallonqiue, hermetique, as well as chyrurgical and fermatie'.

> She also extracts potestates and impetu's, and the three principles of all manner of metals, minerals, animals, vegetals and of mirrh. She makes all kinds of liquor, salts, powders, pills and opiates; whereby she extracts out of the body all

manner of venoms, poysons, plagues, purple spots, measles, great and smallpox with few doses, and in so very short a time as can't be imagin'd not believ'd without one sees it; as also all manner of chollicks of what cause soever, malignant vapours and other, in a moment's time as she has experimented many times.

As well as curing a remarkable range of diseases, she had more to offer.

Besides these and other distempers, this lady preserves youth and beauty. She beautifies without paint and increases radical humour in some and restores it in others, corroborating the spirits, animals or vitals and the whole body, so as to live (God permitting to old age) without any sickness, but on the contrary always lusty, strong and healthy.

She also cured the very condition this lustiness was wont to cause. 'Furthermore, this lady cures the most inveterate distemper that's possible for man or woman to have, which modesty will not permit to name. She cures without seeing them.'

To enjoy newfound youth and beauty to the full, you must be able to see well. So she took care of that too. 'Her Eye Water, so necessary for old people, must also be mentioned, as by the use of it, a person of above 60 years of age may recover as good a sight as a young person.'

Deformities

Another 'gentlewoman' lived 'at the Surgeon's sign, just at the corner of Coventry-court at the Haymarket, near Pickadilly'. She sold preparations to rid the face and body of imperfections. She said:

> God, the author of all things, to make man in love with his wife in the state of innocency, he made her smooth, soft, delicate and fair to intice him; I therefore, that woman might be pleasing to their husbands, and that they might not be offended at their deformities and turn to others, do commend unto you the virtue of an eminent and highly approved 'Balsamick Essence', with several other incomparable cosmeticks, faithfully prepared without mercury.

In the sixteenth century, both arsenic and mercury had been widely used in cosmetics, often with disastrous effects.

> This 'Balsamick Essence' takes away the broadest freckles be they never so long standing, wrinkles, morphew, tan, sunburn or yellowness, in 30 days, and renders the skin plump, soft, fair, bright, smooth and of a lovely colour...
>
> The aged it makes appear fair and young, and preserves beauty to their lives end. 'Tis a most delicate thing to anoint the face with when the smallpox begins to dry, for it certainly prevents all scars and pits.

She also sold a 'super-super-excellent paste for the shaking and trembling of the hands after hard-drinking or otherwise... It also makes them smooth, soft and of a delicate white colour, that although you were to scower brass and pewter and to make coal fires every day, yet nobody will imagine you to do any such drudgery, as hundreds can testify.'

Talc

Talcum powder was used as a face powder, usually in the form of 'Water of Talk and Pearl', along with red lip salve 'that heals all sores and chops in the lips'. Strips of linen or soft leather impregnated with oil, wax and spermaceti – the oil obtained from sperm whales and various cetaceans – were laid on the forehead at night to prevent wrinkles. Complete masks and gloves of the same materials were available.

Beautifying cream

Another gentlewoman promoted her 'Only Delicate Beautifying Cream, [which] is daily sold in great quantities to the Court and the greatest of quality, who continually express their abundant satisfaction in the use of it.' She pointed out that: 'There are many beautiful ladies who have but indifferent hands, and would be overjoyed to make them white, if they knew how… She also hath a curious fine white for the face and neck, entirely without mercury or any such hurtful thing in it;

it being a new thing never before published, one shilling a pot.'
Before the rich began spending time in the South of France in
the 1920s and the fashion for having a suntan came in, a perfectly white skin was all-important.

World's Beautifyer

You could speak to the inventor of the 'World's Beautifyer' at
Nixon's Coffee-house. 'This never failing medicine prepared
without the least mercury of poysonous ingredients, in a week's
time, perfect cures the worst red faces in man or woman,' it
was said.

But you did not have to visit the coffee house. 'If any person of distinction wishes to be waited on at their houses, in
sending notice where they shall be attended,' said the Beautifyer's creator, 'and if any in the country send the colour of their
hair, age and what condition their face is in, to their friend in
town, they may have it delivered to their with direction, they
giving security for the sum agreed upon, the lowest price being
two guineas.'

Water of Pearl

In 1686 Dr Stephen Draper published a handbill addressed to
'Beloved women, who are the admirablest creatures that ever
God created under the canopy of heaven'.

> I commend unto you the virtue of my 'Water of Pearl', with
> several other cosmeticks for the face faithfully prepared
> without mercury.

My 'Water of Pearl' defieth corruption and adorneth the countenance with a lovely rosie complexion, and renders the skin soft, fair, bright, smooth and of a lovely colour. The aged it makes appear young and illustrates beauty to a wonder. Nay, it addeth to nature's masterpiece, a sensible and visible advantage and is but ten shillings a bottle. I also make a Rare Powder, that makes black and yellow teeth as white as ivory and kills scurvey in the gums.

A Water that brings hair on a bald head and an unguent that heals the chops in the lips, and gives them a cherry colour, beautiful to beholders.

Beauty powder

A doctor living at the Blew Ball in Great Knight Rider Street near Doctor's Common sold a 'Famous Powder' called *Arcanum Magnum.*

Being used in time, it prevents the face from ever being wrinkled, though they live to a very old age, and it cures all sorts of red faces. It takes away all heat pimples, sun-burnt and morphew [a leprous or scurfy eruption of the skin or, sometimes, the yellow hue seen in the elderly].

It likewise prevents superfluous hair growing on women's faces and, in short, it adds more lustre and beauty to the face than any other powder or wash ever prepared by any other person, as many persons of quality in England can testify who do daily use it; and all that use it, do admire it above anything to beautify the face.

The original recipe came from the *Arcana*, a treatise by seventeenth-century Italian doctor Lazarus Riverius, who was physician-regent to the king of France. His *Arcanum Magnum*, also known as the 'Golden Extract', was made out of wild thyme, catmint, pennyroyal, bayberries, wild grape, almonds, elderflowers, aniseed, fennel seeds, carrot seeds, cloves, aloe wood, cinnamon and cumin. These were mixed with turpentine, nutmeg oil and Balsam of Peru, and then fermented.

Cures for blushing

In the seventeenth century blushing or any sort of redness of the face was thought to be a sign of melancholia. The cure was to wash your face at night with hare's blood or rub your face with fresh cheese curds when the redness came on – although one would have thought that would be a cause for blushing rather than a cure.

Hair

A hairdresser at the Cross Keys on Ludgate Hill, next to the Rainbow Coffee-house had an 'Extraordinary Essence that preserves the hair in a wonderful manner, and it is of that singular vertue, that it will actually prevent hair shedding after the smallpox, and is to be used instead of Orange Bath of Pomatums'.

Red hair was very much out of fashion in the seventeenth

century, but a gentlewoman who had lived in 'Red Lion Court, but now removed to Racket Court near Fleet Bridge, the third door on the right side', had the answer. 'She can alter red or gray hair to a most delicate light or dark brown, which will continue so for ever without any soil or smooting [smudging].'

She also had a beauty secret 'that no one else hath', which the Queen and court in France use to spend 20,000 gold pieces a year on. 'You may have it from her for half a crown to five pounds a bottle.'

Meanwhile a gentlewoman imported a 'water that will bring hair on a BALD HEAD, if the party be not too old, and an excellent water to make the hair curl'.

CHAPTER NINETEEN

Curious Curers

 F YOU ARE ILL AND want to get well again, you need to have confidence in your doctor. In old England there were a lot of curious characters to put your faith in.

Nicholas Culpeper

The herbalist Nicholas Culpeper (1616–54) had a cure for just about everything. His books, *The Complete Herbal* and *The English Physician*, were still in use in many households in the nineteenth century. To stop a bleeding wound (presumably not one inflicted by the physician himself when bleeding) he recommended: 'Take burnt leather powdered, bole [tree trunk] powders, dragon's blood in power; mix some spirits of win with all these said ingredients and lay it thereon with soft fine lint.' First catch your dragon. Actually, dragon's blood is a resin extruded by the dragon tree, which is used as a homeopathic remedy under the name cinnabar and also to poison cats.

For sore breasts, Culpeper recommended taking a handful

of figs and stamping on them until the kernels broke. Then they should be tempered with fresh grease and applied as hot as the patient can bear. This would 'presently take away the anguish, and if the breast will break, it will break it, else it will cure it without breaking'.

A mixture of bole ammoniac and Venice turpentine applied to the throat from ear to ear with a sheep's leather 'broad as a stay' is the cure for 'the falling down of the almonds of the ears'. These are the tonsils or, sometimes, the lymph glands under the ear.

An egg, hard 'roasted' and peeled, applied to the nape of the neck will stop your eyes watering, while distillate of chopped goat's liver and herbs will clear up your eyesight. You should clean your nose with beetroot juice, while binding up your arms and legs is supposed to cure nosebleeds – or you can blow soot up the nostrils with a funnel. And you can cure polyps in the nose by stuffing a rag soaked in the 'water of adder's-tongue' – also known as hound's-tongue or the dogtooth violet – up the nostril.

Culpeper cured piles with a diet of rosemary and sage eaten with bread and butter, while a plaster of honey and wheat flour was applied to the painful area.

Those with weak stomachs, he said, should avoid anger, sadness, excessive travel, all fried meats, vomiting and eating when they are hot. Avoiding drinking milk or malt liquor for a month and keeping the patient's morning urine in a bottle with a small piece of saffron in it cured jaundice. Culpeper said this remedy and been 'proved a great number of times', but gives no clue on how it is supposed to work. However, he is inordinately pleased that, by this method, he can 'cure the yellow jaundice without medicine, or giving anything to the patient whatsoever'. Other authorities recommended a medicine made by pounding the head of a mad dog and mixing the resulting goo with wine.

Chewing a bit of burnt bread for five minutes, then swallowing half a glass of brandy with 'as much fine sulphur was will lay on a shilling', would kill 'worms or bot-worms in the body', according to Culpeper.

Culpeper also had his more sophisticated versions of the various wart cures that were doing the rounds:

Go into the field and take a black snail, and rub the warts with the snail nine times one way, and then nine times another, and then stick the said snail upon a black thorn, and the warts will waste. I have also known a black snail cure corns, being laid on as a plaster. If you have what is called blood or bleeding warts, then take a piece of raw beef, that never had any salt, and rub them with the same, just in the same manner as you used the snail above mentioned; after this operation is performed, you must bury the piece of beef in the earth.

Other authorities said that the beef must be stolen.

John Wesley

The evangelist and founder of the Methodist movement John Wesley also took a great interest in medicine. In 1747 he published *Primitive Physic*, which lists 288 conditions with 824 cures, some very curious indeed.

Condition 21, 'A Bruise'. Cures:

91. Immediately apply treacle spread on brown paper: Tried.
92. Or, apply a plaister of chopt parsley mixt with butter.
93. Or, electrify the part. This is the quickest cure of all.

Condition 86, 'Blindness'. Cures:

288. Is often cured by cold bathing.
289. Or, by electrifying: tried. This has cured a suffusion [cataract] of 16 years, and a gutta serena [also known as amaurosis – a sudden blindness with no apparent external cause] of 24 years standing.

Condition 144, 'Legs Inflamed'. Cures :

> 451. Apply Fuller's-earth spread on brown paper.
> It seldom fails.
> 452. Or, bruised turnips.
> 455. Use the cold-bath.
> 456. Or, wash in the sea, often and long...
> 459. Or, drink half a pint of cellery whey, morning and
> evening. This has cured the most desperate case.
> 460. Or drink for a month, a decoction of burdock leaves,
> morning and evening: Tried.

Condition 199, 'The Scurvy'. Cure:

> 607. Live on turnips for a month.

Condition 280, 'The Whites' [leucorrhoea, or a white discharge from the vagina]. Cure:

> 795. Live chastely. Feed sparingly. Use exercise constantly.
> Sleep moderately, but never on your back.

Truly God moves in mysterious ways.

It may also be interesting to all pro-lifers to note that John Wesley's Condition 1 is 'Abortion', but then he adds, in parentheses, 'to prevent'.

Like the king of the purgers James Morison, Wesley believed that the body should be regularly stimulated with a 'flesh brush'. He also recommended that people wear as little clothing as possible. This was odd as he maintained that the passions were the cause of most diseases.

Edward Jenner

The English surgeon Edward Jenner is now remembered as the pioneer of vaccination. However, when he first proposed that inoculating patients with cowpox prevented them from contracting the far more dangerous disease of smallpox, he was ridiculed. Indeed the idea was ludicrous to city people. Although Jenner studied under the great surgeon and anatomist John Hunter, he spent most of his life practising as a country doctor in the village of Berkeley in rural Gloucestershire.

During an epidemic of smallpox that hit Gloucestershire in 1788, Jenner noted that those of his patients who worked with cattle did not come down with the disease. He deduced that they were immune because they had suffered from a milder version of the disease called cowpox, which milkmaids and farmers caught from cattle.

To test his theory he took pus from the blisters on the hands of a milkmaid and applied it to two small cuts made on the arm of a young farmer's lad named James Phipps. Six weeks later, Jenner did the same thing with the smallpox virus. If Phipps had died from smallpox, Jenner would have been a murderer. As it was, Phipps survived as the cowpox had made him immune.

In fact, what Jenner was doing was not new. Inoculation, as he called it, had already been discovered by a Dutch physiologist and was widely practised in the Middle East, where liquid

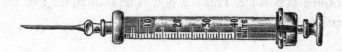

from the pustules of those who had a mild form of the disease was injected into healthy people to boost their immune systems. Lady Mary Wortley Montagu, the wife of the British ambassador to Turkey, had brought the practice back to England in 1721.

Lady Mary's great beauty had been marred by smallpox when she was 26. Then, in Turkey, she had seen the benefits of inoculation and had her six-year-old son inoculated there. Her three-month-old baby daughter was the first person to be inoculated in England. The practice was tested on condemned prisoners in 1723 and some of the upper classes took it up. However, the fad for inoculation proved brief.

In 1798 Jenner published privately *An Inquiry into the Causes and Effects of the Variolae Vaccinae, a Disease Known by the Name of Cow Pox*. Perhaps it was the mention of cows that incited all the ridicule. Caricaturist James Gillray drew a cartoon showing cows coming out of various parts of people's bodies after they had been vaccinated with cowpox.

Despite the mockery, Jenner persevered. Other doctors found that vaccination did work and by 1800 most were using it. Deaths from smallpox plummeted and vaccination spread through Europe and North America, but many still found it curious that you could cure one disease by giving the patient another.

Bedside manner

When it comes to inspiring confidence in patients, the physician's bedside manner is all-important. The thirteenth-century manuscript *De Cautelis Medici* (Tricks for Doctors) recommended straightforward dissembling. 'Suppose you know nothing, say there is an obstruction of the liver,' it advised. 'Perhaps he [the patient] will reply, "Nay master, it is my head or my legs (or other members) that trouble me." Repeat that it comes from the liver or stomach. Especially use the word obstruction as patients do not understand it.'

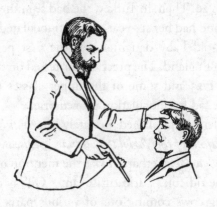

The great philosopher

In 1782 the self-styled 'greatest philosopher in this kingdom since Isaac Newton' set up shop at 22 Piccadilly. His name was Gustavus Katterfelto and he gave 'demonstrations' of 'philosophy, mathematics, optics, magnetism, electricity, chemistry, pneumatics, hydraulics, poetry, styangraphy, palenchics and caprimantic arts'. However, I can find no reference to these last three outside Mr Katterfelto's lively imagination. Front seats were three shillings (15p), second seats two shillings and back seats one shilling, and shows ran from eight in the morning to six in the evening.

Katterfelto claimed to have performed before the Queen of

Hungary, the Empress of Russia and the kings of Prussia, Sweden, Denmark and Poland. Fashionable people turned out to see him and, it was said, even the King took an interest. But then on 3 June 1782, the *Morning Post* announced that 'Mr Katterfelto was taken very ill with the very alarming disorder that at present rages throughout this metropolis. The symptoms were a great weakness of the limbs, a swimming in the head and a shivering of the whole body.'

However, the great philosopher was not to be laid low by a simple illness. He consulted the works of one Dr Bato and tried his medicines. According to the newspaper:

> He found himself cured in 12 hours. Several persons have since been convinced of the amazing efficacity of this medicine and now Mr Katterfelto, as a philosopher and a philanthropist, gives the public notice that he has prepared a large quality of the above invaluable medicine, which will be sold (by him only), at the low price of five shillings [25p] per bottle, signed and sealed by Mr Katterfelto.

In his advertisement, Katterfelto claimed that the concoction had 'cured many thousand persons of the late influenza'.

It would be easy to dismiss Katterfelto as a quack, but among the inventions he demonstrated was a 'solar microscope'. Through it 'those insects which caused the late influenza will be seen as large as birds, and in a drop of water the size of a pin's head, there will be seen 50,000 insects; the same in beer, milk, vinegar, flour, blood, cheese, etc.' This is eight years before Louis Pasteur and Joseph Lister came up with the idea that diseases were caused by germs.

Oxford doctors

'At the Angel and Crown in Basing-lane, being the second turning on the left hand in Bread-street from Cheapside, dwelt a physician, a graduate in the University of Oxford and a member of the College of Physicians in London.'

This distinguished medical man 'has a pill prepared with wholesome ingredients and of great vertue, that it ought not to be concealed. These pills will take away all scabs in the head and face and pains in the head, arms or legs and prevent much danger, and are to be bought at my house in Basing-lane from one shilling and sixpence [8p]'.

However, another physician who claimed to be 'an Oxford doctor' does not inspire such confidence, even though his handbill was headed by a Greek quotation. The services he offered were common enough. He claimed his 'Oxon Pills against scurvy, dropsie and colt evil exceed all other medicines and are sixpence a box'. Colt evil was a swelling of the sheath of the penis thought to be common in young male horses, or perhaps good old-fashioned priapism.

This Oxonian also doubled as a dentist: 'He draws teeth or stumps with ease and safety,' and as a barber-surgeon: 'He lets blood neatly and issues or setons he curiously makes, for twopence each and welcome!' (Setons are pieces of thread or tape drawn through the skin to maintain an issue or opening for the discharge of pus, or they are drawn through a sinus or cavity to prevent it healing up. I would not want this 'curiously' done – though 'curiously' here means carefully, skilfully or accurately – even at less than 1p a go.) He also taught 'writing, arithmetick, Latin, Greek and Hebrew, at reasonable rates by the great [fixed amount of work], or two-pence, each of them by the week'.

This is all pretty impressive. What lets him down, though, is his address. Those interested in consulting him were told to 'RAPAIR TO THE OXFORD DOCTOR AT THE FLEET PRISON, near Fleet-bridge, London.'

He concluded his handbill by claiming that he was 'Lately a Fellow of Arx-cerer Collge [sic], Oxon', where they neglected to teach him to spell.

The Secret Cabinet

The College of Physicians had set up its dispensary in Warwick Lane in 1698 'to reform the abuses of the apothecaries'. However, it soon found it had a rival – 'A New Dispensary to save Patient's money and the Publick health'. The organisers explained:

This dispensary is not set on foot by a Society of Physicians, but is where instead of large fees, long bills and quacks more dangerous practice, all persons, in what circumstances whatsoever managed, with as much safety and judgment and integrity, as if they had the advice of a whole Colledge, but with much less expense than the meanest pretender. For which purpose the Society have provided a collection of the choicest specifics yet known, which we call our SECRET CABINET adapted to all diseases. Therefore be it known, we have always ready, The 'Green Catharick Elixir', far exceeding any other for gripes and cholick; The 'Hysterical Tincture'; The 'Great Balsamick Spirit'; The 'White Cadialgick Powder', which in all cases excels Crab's eyes, Pearl, Coral

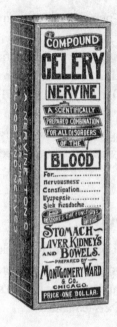

and all the Testaceous Powders; The 'Grey Ointment' and 'The Black Cerecloth' or Plaister for the Rickets call'd 'The Jewel', a secret left by a famous Jew, who got a vast estate by it, which since his death had been communicated to one of the society as the most valuable thing in the world for wounds.

Note. The Society have taken care to provided particular specificks for all the modish diseases.

The use of 'modish' here is interesting, as if some condition was this season's latest must-have disease.

Seventh sons

In the seventeenth century, belief in the occult healing power of the seventh son of a seventh son persisted. One handbill advertised:

There is newly arrived in London an UNBORN DOCTOR, THE SEVENTH SON OF A SEVENTH SON, who, (by God's blessing on his studies) and more than 27 years travels with most famous and eminent physicians has obtained to be an able chymical physician, oculist and chyrurgical operator.

He hath made a large demonstration of his great abilities in several kingdoms, and as well in hospitals and war-like expeditions as in other places, for he hath obtained such a physical method as never was in England before for the cure of all curable distempers in bodies of men, women and children. He hath cured many in his travels of very sad and deplorable diseases, which had been left off by learned physicians and chyrurgions as to be incurable, as he can show by testimonials from several electorial princes, dukes and persons of quality.

As well as curing the usual range of distempers, he also had the ability to treat 'epilepsy, rickets, madness and megrims [migraine or general low spirits]'.

As a chyrurgical operator, this Unborn Doctor is able to take from the eyes, all pin-webs [blisters on the eye-ball] and cataracts in a quarter of an hour. He cures, to a wonder, those which are deaf even if for more than 20 years. He hath also a great secret for the cure of crooked children and morbus gallicus, a method never in England till now.

It is not clear how he practised – or how he was even alive – if he was 'unborn'.

Another seventh son and 'Unborn Doctor' also fancied himself as a poet. His handbill read:

to see Now follow a catalogue of what he'll do,
Be your distemper old or new.
First, morbus gallicus, you may be sure,
He with speed will soundly cure,
And as for the gout, if any can,
He'll ease or cure with any man;
But I confess unto you all,
It is the Master of Physician Hall,
And as for the stone,

If in the bladder it dissolveth not,
He safely cuts it out,
And cures the patient you need not doubt.
Now as for palsy, fever and all aching pains,
He'll cure in limbs, nerves, joints and veins.
For wounds, tumours, cancers and running sores,
In the year, he cures many scores.
Now to all women he is a friend,
If they be sick or ill, he doth them mend,
And as for children, of what e're they ail,
To cure them he'll never fail.
And as for those that deaf may be,
Or lost their sight and cannot see,
He by art doth them restore,
Be they rich or be they poor;
For every one of each degree,
That deaf and blind have been,
He hath brought to hear agen
Or see as well as e'en.
So 'tis for that very thing,
His fame in England now do ring.
All ye that of cure do stand in need,
Make haste and go to him with speed;
For be ye poor, sick, lame or blind,
He'll on his word, to you be kind.
So to conclude and make an end,
I to you this paper send
That you may see God's gift is great to me,
By which I cause the lame to go
And the blind to see.

Cradle and Coffin

From 1665 to 1680, Gilbert Anderson practised in Cross Street, St Giles, under the sign of the Cradle and Coffin – which must have inspired confidence in his patients. His handbill was headed: 'All praise and glory to be given to God alone.' It goes on to say that:

> ... he hath travell'd throughout the most part of the known world, and so acquired the most rare secrets of physick and chyrurgery during 35 years, 12 of which he spent in the quality of chyrurgeon to a ship, in the wars of Candia, in which time he never made a voyage without fighting; and yet was so happy in his undertaking, that he never dismembered any man, neither did any dye under the cure of their wounds; but on the contrary, he cured many that were to have been dismember'd by others.

Unlike many of his contemporaries, Anderson had no cure-all pills or potions.

He hath no remedies that cure all diseases, but he hath for each several disease a proper remedy, and undertakes to cure rheums that fall from the head to the teeth, the black and blue marks caused by blows, in 48 hours, and hath a plaister for sciatica or huckle-bone [bone of the hip] gout which will banish all the pain in a wonderful short time.

Anderson also made a pledge to his patients. 'He solemnly promises in the presence of Almighty God and the Holy Host of Heaven, not to undertake any but such as he hath good hopes are curable by him.'

South Sea Bubble

The eighteenth-century financial scam the South Sea Bubble caused many British investors a headache, but it has helped cure people ever since. It gave London bookseller Thomas Guy the £300,000 he needed to establish Guy's Hospital, which opened in Southwark in 1726, and is thought to be the last general hospital to have been endowed in full by one person.

Holland – home of medical learning

English doctors could not cure all the curious complains that were going about and needed help from abroad. In the seventeenth century, Holland was seen as the home of medical learning and a graduate of the University of Leyden set up his surgery in 'Crutchet-Fryers near Aldgate, between two wine-coopers, over against the Three Golden Anchors, where you shall see a hatch at the entry door and a Lanthorn hung over it'. According to his handbill:

> He can do such cures, that there is not any example of the like extant, either in books or in the memory of men, for he hath cured even those that had all their guts fallen that could not be thrust back by others, although they had hanged up the poor patient by the feet as if it had been an ox or a calf.

And he was honest. 'Now, for to let the world know his integrity and upright and honest dealing, he maketh his agreement; that he will not have any money for his pains and medicines until half a year after the patient hath been perfectly cured.'

German doctors

German practitioners were also much in demand in the seventeenth and eighteenth centuries. One 'German doctor and surgeon' worked out of the Boot and Spatterdash – a spatterdash being a long gaiter or leather legging designed to keep the trouser leg or stocking from being spattered especially when riding. The word was later abbreviated to the more familiar 'spat'.

The Boot and Spatterdash was in Long Acre near the junction with Drury Lane, just two doors from the Vine Tavern, where many of the famous physicians of the time met. It was celebrated in Sir Samuel Garth's poem 'The Dispensary', which was first published in 1699 to celebrate the opening of the Royal College of Physicians' dispensary the year before.

Herr Doctor believed he was more than a match for any of the medical men of the day. 'By the blessing of God on his great pains, travels and experience, [he] hath had wonderful success.' He could 'recover and give sight to the blind in a moment, cure hair-lips in six days, and the cancer of the breast or any other part of the body'.

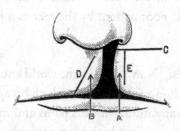

Ladies need not be modest. 'If any woman be unwilling to speak to me, they may have the conveniency of speaking to my wife, who is expert in all women's distempers. As to gouty pains or shrinking of the sinews, I dare presume, few have arriv'd to the perfection in this cure as myself.'

Poet practitioner

A number of medical men turned their hands to writing poetry, perhaps believing that it would inspire confidence in patients if they showed themselves to be all-rounders in the world of learning. One such was Thomas Saffold, who obtained a licence to practise medicine from the Bishop of London, as the law at that time required, on 4 September 1674. He set up shop as 'an approved and licensed physician and student in astrology'.

He turned to poetry for the purposes of advertising. His verse was handed out on handbills along Cheapside, Fleet Street, the Strand, Whitehall and St James's. One read:

THE SICK MAY HAVE ADVICE FOR NOTHING
And good medicines cheap, if so they please,
For to cure any curable disease.
It's Saffold's Pills much better than the rest,
Deservedly have gain'd the name of Best;
In curing by the cause, quite purging out
Of scurvy, French-pox, agues, stone and gout.
The head, stomach, belly and the reins [kidneys], they
Will cleanse and cure, while you may work or play.
His pills have often, to their maker's praise,
Cur'd in all weathers, yea in the dog-days.
In short no purging med'cine is made, can
Cure more diseases in man or wo-man,
Than his cheap pills, but three shillings a box,
A sure cure for the running reins and pox.
Each box contains thirty-six pills, I'm sure
As good as e're were made, scurvy to cure.
The half box, eighteen pills for eighteen pence,
Though 'tis too cheep in any man's own sense.

For those who had difficulty swallowing pills, there was an elixir or liquor that sold at half a crown (13p) a bottle and would cure 'dropsie, agues, stone and gout, as well as the disease too much in fashion' – that is, the French pox. He said that those who had tried:

His best pills, rare elixir and powder,
Do each day praise him lowder and lowder.

Saffold did not claim that he could cure in all cases. Aware of his limitations, he wrote:

He can cure when God Almighty pleases,
But cannot protect against all diseases,
If men will live intemperate and sin,
He cannot help't if they be sick agen.
This great truth unto the world he'll tell
None can cure sooner, who cures half so well.

In 1691 Saffold fell ill. Rejecting the help of a physician, he put his faith in his own pills and died on 12 May. His death itself was the subject of verse, with one satirist writing:

For he when sick refuse all doctor's aid
And only to his pills devotion paid;
Yet it was surely a most sad disaster
The SAWCY PILLS at last should KILL THEIR MASTER.
Even his epitaph showed little respect:
Here lyes the corps of Thomas Saffold,
By death, in spite of physick, baffl'd…
Now death does poet, doctor crowd
Within the limits of a shroud.

Another case

Saffold's place was quickly taken by John Case, who was a well-known writer and compiler of astrological almanacs, as well as learned titles. He gilded Saffold's Black Ball and announced:

At the Golden Ball and Lillies Head
John Case yet lives, though Saffold's dead.
Under the Golden Ball, he hung a sign which read:
Within this place
Lives Doctor Case.

The *Tatler* magazine said: 'Case made more money by this couplet, than Dryden made by all his poetical works put together.'

In 1695 Case published *Compendium Anataomicum nova methodo institutum*, which discussed the ideas of William Harvey and Reinier de Graaf, pioneers in the study of the pancreas and the ovaries. It won him fame as a medical writer.

Like Safford, 'Case offers the poor, sore, sick and lame, advice for nothing, and proper medicines for every particular distemper at reasonable rates.' He offered an extra service. 'He doth also, with great certainty and privacy, resolve all manner of lawful questions according to the rules of Christian astrology.' He also claimed to be a 'spagyrick physician' – 'spagyrick' is another name for the science of alchemy.

'An approved practitioner in that famous science of physick in 1672,' Case boasted, 'and both before and since, has been an industrious inquirer into the secrets of spagyrick or chymical art. He has a laboratory of his own in this city in the said art and at length by the blessing of God attained a most noble

Universal Medicine, which he has thought fit to call by the name of *Mundus Sanitatus*, the operations of which are the wonder of the world, price two shillings and six pence [13p], very proper. The *Pilula Cathartica*, the true *Medicarem Universale*, *Gutta Stipitica Miraculum Mundi*, the world's wonder for inward wounds, *Liquor Diuretica* and *Analepticus*, and the cordial draught or wonderful Elixir.'

He also advertised his services by handing out his verse in handbills. One read:

> All yet that are of Venus race,
> Apply yourselves to Dr Case;
> Who with a box or two of pills,
> Will soon remove your painful ills.

However, Case came to rely more on astrology. His last book, *The Angelical Guide, showing men and women their lott or Chaunce in this Elementary*, published in 1697, confines itself to astrology and fortune telling.

Seeing stars

Many poet practitioners dabbled in astrology, as did the doctor who practised 'nearby in Baldwin's Court, Holborn, at the sign of the Moon and Stars in Leopard's-court… from eight in the morning until seven at night'. He sold 'Cephalick Powder, a present remedy for all diseases of the head proceeding from the colds or excess of humours, price sixpence a paper'. His handbill concluded:

Would you your minds free from each labouring doubt,
The future state of your disease find out?
Then WHEN and HOW of things to come explore,
Shall you grow rich or (God forbid) be poor?
Are you fall'n sick or grievous pains endure?
He'll tell the best and speedi'st way to cure.
If good to marry, if the charming soul
That wounds your heart, will ever make it whole;
Ask but the doctor, you shall truly know
What in each thing the ruling stars will do.

Despite the distinguished quality of his verse, this man did not speak English. A graduate of the University of Louvain in Brabant, now in Belgium, he could only speak to his patients in Latin or French.

Notwithstanding, his wife was also in the business, selling 'excellent beautifying washes at one shilling a bottle, and has proper remedies for distempers incident to the female sex'. He was, of course, basically an astrologer, and asked: 'Those that can procure the time of their birth are desired to bring it with them, because some questions are best answer'd and some diseases best discover'd, by the party's nativity.'

Gilding the Lilly

Not all doctor-astrologers had such distinguished backgrounds. William Lilly came to London from Leicestershire as a boy to seek his fortune. He worked as a servant to Gilbert Wright, performing 'all manner of drudgeries, such as cleaning the shoes, carrying water and scraping the trenchers [boards for serving food on]'. Surviving the plague of 1625, he began to study medicine and astrology, and soon claimed that he could diagnose a disease by the stars.

After publishing a series of books and astrological almanacs, he moved to Hersham in Surrey in 1665, where he obtained a licence from the Archbishop of Canterbury to practise medicine. Every Saturday he would ride into Kingston-upon-Thames to distribute medical advice and medicine free to the poor. When he died in 1681 and was buried in Walton Church, his friend Elias Ashmole, founder of the Ashmolean Museum in Oxford, donated the marble slab covering his grave.

Big-wigs

In the eighteenth century there was doctor named Colonel Dalmahoy who was famous for the size of his wig, along with

his face-washes, love-philtres and charms. A popular ballad of
the day began:

> If you would see a noble wig,
> And in that wig a man look big,
> To Ludgate Hill repair, my joy,
> And gaze of Col'nel Dalmahoy.

When he died, he was commemorated in verse.

> Dalmahoy sold infusions and lotions,
> Decoctions and gargles and pills,
> Electuaries, powders and potions,
> Spermanceti, salts, scammoy, squills.

> Horse-aloes, burnt alum, agaric,
> Balm, benzoin, blood-stone and dill,
> Castor, camphor, and acid tartaric
> With 'specifics' for every ill.

> But with all his 'specifics' in store,
> Death on Dalmahoy one day did pop;
> And although he had doctors a score,
> Made Dalmahoy shut up shop.

Dalmahoy was following in the footsteps of Dr Lionel Lockyer and Will Atkins, a doctor who lived at the Old Bailey during the reign of Charles II. On his walks to visit his patients he
would carry a fancy cane and on his head he had a huge wig

that was frizzed out to such dimensions that he could not wear a hat. One contemporary description ran:

> … to make him look more big,
> Had on a large, grave, decent, three-tailed wig;
> His clothes full-trimmed, with button holes behind,
> Stiff were the skirts, with buckram stoutly lined,
> The cloth-cut velvet, or more reverend black,
> Full-made and powder'd half-way down his back.

This must have inspired confidence as it was very much the fashion for doctors to wear full wigs at the time.

Nearly reviving the dead

The above-mentioned Atkins subscribed to the common belief that the more drugs a preparation contained the better. He boasted that the 30 ingredients he used in his patent concoction, 'all calculated to ease the complaint'. But this was easily outstripped by the 62 ingredients in the *Elixir Vitae* made by Salvator Winter, who lived nearby at the 'sign of St Paul's Head, in New King-street, between Long-acre and St Giles-in-the-fields, near Covent Garden'. And he was living proof that it worked. 'He always carries in his pocket at days, and at night under his pillow,' his *Elixir* and when he found himself 'distempered, he taketh a spoonful or two, according as need requireth'. Consequently, he has lived to '98 years of age yet by the blessing of God, [and] finds himself in health as strong as anyone of 50'. However, it is unlikely that anyone could have checked up on this as Winters came from Naples.

His *Elixir*, he said, cured catarrhs, consumption, French pox and 'hath such force and vigour that if it were possible it would revive the dead, were that not a secret reserved to God only'. Winter also boasted that his *Elixir* got a write-up by 'The Most Learned and Honourable of Worthy Memory Sir Kenelm Digby', a founder member of the Royal Society. The rave review, according to Winter, was that his 'Miraculous *Elixir Vitae*... never doth harm, but assuredly doth good.' He also pointed out in his handbill that though there was a report abroad 'THAT HE IS DEAD, but he wishes it to be known THAT HE IS VERY MUCH ALIVE and of so great an age'.

Pisse-prophets

The examination of the urine had always been an important diagnostic tool. As far back as the thirteenth century there was a textbook on the subject called *De Urinas*. By the seventeenth century this had developed into the full-blown discipline known as uroscopy. Specialists known as 'pisse-prophets' would indulge in 'urine-gazing', making detailed diagnoses from the colour, smell and even taste of the patient's urine. They advertised their practice by hanging a chamber pot outside their premises.

The great advantage these urologists had was that they could offer a discreet service, making remote diagnoses from a sample brought by a friend or servant. Their powers were truly remarkable. When a woman had brought a sample of her husband's urine to one practitioner, the urine-gazer quickly spotted some blood in it.

'The party hath received some internal hurt,' he said. The

wife agreed. The pisse-prophet soon ascertained that the woman's husband had fallen down stairs.

'How many pair of stairs did he fall down?' she asked mischievously.

When the urologist had found out where the woman lived, he hazarded a guess.

'Two pairs of stairs,' he said.

'Nay, you are out in your art,' she said. 'He fell down three storeys.'

The expert then asked the woman whether the urine he had 'cast' was all that her husband had passed that morning. The women said no, she had spilt some.

'That, woman,' said the pisse-prophet, 'was the business that made me mistake.'

Skill in urines

There was a 'doctor of physick well-known for his successful practice in the City of London, who lived in the Haymarket by Charing-cross, at the sign of the Half Moon, next the Nag's Head Tavern, being the Balcony Room, one pair of stairs', who took as his motto 'deo adjuvante'. This means 'with God's help' or 'God help us', which is not very reassuring.

However, he claimed 'an admirable skill in urines, though ignorants dispise it, yet from which the learned know the truest indications of occult diseases'.

Again it would be easy to dismiss this man as a piss-taker, but he pioneered a treatment for neurasthenia and tuberculosis that was only fully established centuries later. 'For melancholy persons inclining to distraction or such that are consumption,' he wrote, 'he hath a large country house with gardens, being excellent air, within a mile of town, where the doctor is daily to give advice and what physick is most necessary for recovery, at easie rates.'

The Globe and Urinal

Another 'licensed and legal practitioner in physick and surgery' worked under the sign of the 'Globe and Urinal at the corner house next the square in Baldwin's Gardens near Holbourn, the third turning from Leather-lane and third from Gray's Inn'. I think that, with that sign, it would be safe to assume that he was a pisse-prophet – because if the 'Globe and Urinal' is a pub sign, I don't want to drink there.

He sold the 'Famous Arconum Pill, which he doth assure is free from mercury and is a perfect cure for *morbus gallicus*'. He also described himself as 'a friend to the diseased and his remedy, which also cureth the scurvy and all rheumatick pains, may be taken in any season by sea or land'.

He offered a full range of other services. 'Take notice,' he said, 'in short, that this artist cureth all diseases curable, and he is the only man in town for curing the King's Evil, cancer and ulcers. He can also take away all webs, pearls, spots, sparks, clouds and films from the eyes, and coutheth cataracts if occasion be.'

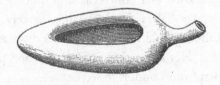

Hearing for the deaf

The Searl family of Pye Corner, over against the Golden Ball by West Smithfield, specialised in curing deafness. The last of the line, Margaret Searl, distributed a handbill which said that 'she is still to be found at Pye Corner (although it is reported that I was dead by some pretenders to deceive the world) where I am ready, upon any occasion of the nature to serve such as apply themselves to me, being the survivor of my father Edmund Searl, and of my late husband, Samuel Searl'.

This sounds suspiciously as though she married her brother, but no matter. She could cure deafness as 'her father had practised this art about 38 years and communicated the secret to her only, who practis'd it with him in his lifetime'. Sadly, the cure died with her.

Bonesetting

Bonesetting was another traditional skill often passed from parent to offspring, and in the eighteenth century one particular female bonesetter came to fame. Her name was Sarah Wallin and she was the daughter of a bonesetter who lived in Hindon, Wiltshire.

Looking for a little excitement, Sarah left the village and travelled around the country. She settled in Epsom, Surrey, where she practised as a bonesetter and quickly acquired the nickname 'Crazy Sally'. She was large, fiercely ugly and so strong that she was said to be able to set a dislocated shoulder single-handed. Her reputation spread and soon patients were coming down from London to see her.

On 17 August 1736, Sarah married Hill Mapp, footman to a mercer who sold expensive fabrics on Ludgate Hill in London. A week after the wedding he ran off with 100 guineas. She does not seem to have missed him or the money.

She was in such great demand that she would travel up to London in her coach and four, accompanied by liveried footmen and outriders. Once she was mistaken for an unpopular German noblewoman in Old Kent Road. When a menacing crowd surrounded her coach, she simply pulled down the window and shouted: 'Damn your bloods. Don't you know me? I'm Mrs Mapp, the bonesetter.'

The crowd then gave her a great cheer and she went on her way unmolested.

Twice a week she saw patients at the Grecian Coffee-house. According to *Gentlemen's Magazine* of October 1736, she operated there in front of Sir Hans Sloane. In his presence, she cured 'a man of Wardour Street, whose back had been broken nine years and stuck out two inches. A niece of Sir Hans Sloane who was in like condition, was cured, also a gentleman who went with one shoe heel six inches high, having been lame twenty years of his hip and knee, whom she sent straight and brought his leg down even with the other.'

William Hogarth included her in his print *The Undertaker's Arms of Consultation of Physicians*, and a contemporary account said:

The cures of the woman bone-setting of Epsom are too many to be enumerated; her bandages are extraordinarily neat and her dexterity is reducing dislocations and setting fractured bones wonderful. The lame come to her daily and she gets a great deal of money, persons of quality who attend her operations, making her presents.

She was so rich and famous that a race at Epsom was run in her name, which she endowed with a gold plate worth ten guineas as a prize. The first heat was won by a mare named 'Mrs Mapp'. She was so delighted that she gave the jockey a guinea, and promised to make it a hundred if he won. He lost.

Perhaps she did miss her husband after all. She began drinking heavily, was deserted by friends and patients, and died in poverty in lodgings off Seven Dials.

Rupture specialist

H. Hippen, who lived at the 'Crown and Golden Ball on London Bridge, next door to the coffee-house, near St Magnus' Church', specialised in the cure of ruptures and claimed to offer a unique service. 'By the blessing of God and his great study, travels and experience,' he said, 'he hath at last attained to that, which many of our forefathers of the same profession have sought for, but never so completely found, as (God be praised) he hath; and has had wonderful success in cure of the disease.'

Sufferers were warned to 'defer not the time but come over to him before it is too late'. And they should not worry about the cost. He was not in business to profit from the unfortunate or to make a great deal of money.

No, in truth he is in none of those, and he will give you to understand his agreement with all his afflicted patients; he takes no money for his trouble or medicines, till a quarter of a year after the cure is performed, and then, as a reward for the same, he requires the sum of 40 shillings [£2, or £200 in today's money] or those who are not able, 30 shillings. FOR THOSE THAT HAVE NO MONEY AND DESIRE IT FOR GOD'S SAKE, HE WILL CURE GRATIS.

Trusses

Bartlett of Goodmans Fields sold 'spring trusses, collar, swings and other inventions from the Golden Ball by the tavern in Prescot street, and the Golden Ball and Naked Boys against the Rainbow Coffee-house'. He claimed that his trusses could cure 'men from 40 to 79 of this malady, and reduce desperate ruptures in a few minutes, likely to be moral in a few hours'. 'I can make the weak strong, and the crooked straight,' he boasted.

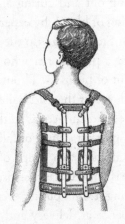

Putting children straight

Nathaniel Baker, who lived at the Golden Spurr in Round Court in St Martin's-Legrand near Newgate Street, could also put the crooked straight. He had 'lately come to England (by the Help of God) and undertakes to set all children straight that are growing awry, either in body, legs or feet'.

His credentials were impressive. 'It has been my business for upwards of 30 years having perfected the cure of some hundreds, who for want of timely application, would have been deformed and cripples all days of their lives,' he said. 'The sooner I am applied the better. I do it without putting to any pain.'

The first Master Corn-cutter of old England

One of the best-known chiropodists of the seventeenth century was Thomas Smith of King Street, who claimed to being the 'first Master Corn-cutter of England'. He said he had 'learnt the art of taking out and curing all manner of corns without pain or drawing of blood, by experience and ingenuity in a way no man in England can do the like'.

However, there was a practitioner who aimed to put our Master Corn-cutter out of business. Thomas Shadells of Sea-Coall Lane in Bear Alley near the Old Bailey claimed that 'he hath an infallible remedy to cure corns so that they will never grow or offend again, putting a drop of falling spittle upon a thin bit of leather, and then two drops of the bottle, every morning till the bottle is out. He has likewise a ball for the bottoms of the feet, putting it on a plaster every week till cured. He sells it for three pence at delivery and three pence when cured... I also cut corns to all Gentlemen's satisfaction. I have a green plaister for a hard corn and a white plaister for a soft corn, both of them one pence.'

CHAPTER TWENTY

Crazy Quacks

LONGSIDE UNSCIENTIFIC and probably incompetent doctors, there were out-and-out quacks. However, they had their place in the medical profession too – if only as entertainers who had the cure for low spirits.

Mountebanks

Of course, there were some in the profession who could not stand them. *The Anatomies of the True Physician and Counterfeit Mountebanks* published in 1605 paints a damning picture:

> The whole Rable of these quack-Saluers are of a base wit and perverse. They for the most part are the abject and sordidous scumme and refuse of the people, who having run away from their trades and occupations leane in a corner to get their livings by killing men, and if we… bring them to light, which like owls they cannot abide, they will appear to be runagate Jews, the cut-throats and robbers of Christians, slow-bellied

monks who had made escape from their cloisters, Simoniacal and perjured shavelings, buy St John-lack-Latins, thrasonical and unlettered chemists, shifting and outcast pettifoggers, light-headed and trivial druggers and apothecaries, sun-shunning night-birds and corner creepers, dull-pated and base mechanics, stage players, jugglers, pedlars, prittle-prattling and cogging cavaliers, bragging soldiers, lazy clowns, one-eyed and lamed fencers, toothless and tattle old wives, chattering char-women and nurse-keepers, scape-Tyburns, dog-leeches and suchlike baggage... In the next rank, to second this goodly troupe, follow poisoners, enchanters, wizards, fortune tellers, magicians, witches and hags.

Orvietan and the green salve

There was nothing a quack liked better than a public stage. During the Restoration, one Dr Pontaeus appeared, claiming that his potion 'Orvietan' was the antidote to all poisons and that his 'green salve' would heal any wound. To prove his claims, he issued a challenge to the learned physicians of Oxford. 'If they would prepare the rankest poison they could contrive,' he said, 'he would undertake that one of his servants should swallow it, and after taking a dose of his Orvietan, he would recover, and so prove the value of his antidote.'

Oxford's doctors took up the challenge and prepared a dose of '*aqua fortis*' – nitric acid. On stage, the servant duly swal-lowed it, fell down dead and was carried off. However, the next day he appeared again, apparently none the worse for wear.

Dr Harris, physician-in-ordinary to Charles II, explained how this was done. The servant had swallowed two or three pounds of butter, which protected the inside of his mouth and his stomach with a thick layer of grease. After he was carried off stage, Pontaeus dosed him with more butter and warm water. This induced vomiting and the servant brought the nitric acid up again, leaving him unharmed. Do not try this at home.

There was a similar demonstration of Pontaeus's Green Salve. On stage his assistant appeared to wash his hands in a ladle-full of molten lead. When he pulled his hands out of the bowl, they appeared to be terribly burned. Ponteaus applied some of his green salve and bandaged them up. Next day, the assistant appeared without the bandages and his hands miraculously intact. This was because the ladle had not contained molten lead at all, but warm mercury. The inside of the bowl was covered in red paint and the assistant had red dye hidden between his fingers, which he rubbed over his hands while they were in the quicksilver.

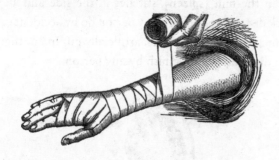

Multi-talented medic

A medical man, apparently, first brought Orvietan to England from Orvieto and it did the rounds. Another user was Cornelius à Tilbourn who claimed in his advertising literature to be the 'sworn chyrurgeon' to the king. He said he had 'the only true Orvietan that expelled vast quantity of poyson before King Charles II, for which I received from that courteous prince, [a] gold medal and chain. I dispose of it from half a crown the box, to five shillings, and so what quantity or price you please.'

Unusually, Tilbourn operated on a no-cure, no-pay basis, and he even gave his patients food and lodgings while undergoing treatment. His handbill carried five coats of arms and claimed that he practised 'By their Majesties Special License and Authority'. It goes on to list the services he provided:

I perform all manual operations, as the stone in the bladder or kidneys, by cutting or by particular medicines. I recover and give sight to the blind. I restore sight in a moment. I cure deafness (if curable). I cure vomiting, rising of the vapours, pain in the milt [spleen], stitches in the side and all scorbutick distempers. I can, if any person do by accident or misfortune, lose one of his eyes, artificially put in another, not to be discerned as a blemish by any person.

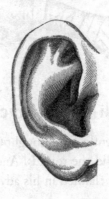

He gives accounts of cures he has 'lately performed on persons of quality':

> Sir Richard Greeneway, troubled with the stone, was speedily cured by me. John Owen, Esquire, who so honourably served his late Majesty in the Dutch engagements and had five or six ulcerated holes in his legs, occasioned by splinters, and at first but ill patcht up: in less than six weeks, I made him sound and well. The Lady Ann Seymoure, that had a lameness in her limbs, that she was forced to keep to her bed for four years, was cured by me in seven weeks time, and I also cured a cancerated lip of Sir John Andrews at St James's.

Then came Tilbourn's triumph.

> Mr Christopher Shelly hard by Cupid's Bridge in Lambeth was brought to me in a chair, deprived of all his limbs, uncapable of moving hand or foot as (by the blessing of God) perfectly cured by me, to the admiration of all. I could mention a great many more which I have cured, but the paper being too little. VIVANT REX ET REGINA.

Later Tilbourn practised as an oculist, and his new handbill said that by his 'great diligence and study, he hath lately found out some admirable remedies which was never yet made publick, for weak or dim sight occasioned by age or otherwise, and bring them to see well without spectacles in a week's time, although they have used them 20 years before'. He also said that he could take off all 'pearls, pins, webs, cataracts, both white and black, and skins of all kinds, and gives immediate sight to those that are termed stone-blind'.

Tilbourn later changed his name and, although continuing to practise his no-cure, no-pay policy, considerably broadened the conditions he would treat.

Now the agreement I make with everyone is, I shall not require one farthing till they have been cured half a year, so well, only I shall require your names and the places of your abode when the half-year is expired. I do cure all persons that have been at Venus sports of the French, Italian, Indian, High Dutch, English or Spanish variety. If any person hath the scurvy in the mouth or blacking teeth, I can clean them, although they be black as pitch, and make them extraordinary white.

Tilbourn seems to have lived on through the brief reign of James II and the Glorious Revolution to become 'privileged by our Gracious Sovereign Lord and Lady, King William and Queen Mary'.

Tilbourn II

A few years later Dr James Tilbourn went into business in London. He may have been related to Cornelius, although he claimed to be 'a very expert, famous outlandish doctor and citizen of Hambourgh, and now arrived in London, and hath brought wonderful art with him, which he hath found through long seeking-for and travelling through many kingdoms'.

He was, he said, 'famous through Germany and Holland,

Brabant [Belgium], France and Italy and is now living at the Black Swan in St Giles in the Fields, over against Drury-lane end, where you shall see at night three lanthorns with candles burning in them upon the balcony'. So he had the same MO as his namesake. 'He may be spoke with, all alone, from eight of the clock in the morning till ten at night, desiring you to be careful for your own benefit not to mistake the place, because there is a new person that is lately come over and hath presumed to make use of the bill and piece which I did formerly make use of.' According to his handbill he offered a number of services:

First, he cures the French pox, with all its dependents. Secondly, he takes away all pains in the shoulders, arms and bones, therefore all ye that are troubled come to him before you are spoiled by others, for this secret art was never heard of or seen by any as by him.

If any have anchored in a strange harbour, fearing to have received damage, let them come to him.

Lastly, he helps them that have lost their nature and cherish up those sad'ned spirits of a marrye'd man, by what occasion soever they have lost it, and does quicken them again as a rose that had received the summer's dew.

Pimple-Pamplins

Thomas Rand dispensed his cures from a stage set up in Moorfields, where he claimed to 'sell to the rich but give to the poor'. When he attracted a sufficiently large crowd, he would ask his audience: 'Is there any old woman amongst you troubled with the Pimple-Pamplins, whose skin is too short for their bodies?'

Not a condition familiar today. 'See, here is my "Anti-pampha-stick Powder" or my "Sovereign Carminick", which discharges ventiferous humours of what kind soever and will reduce you to soundness of body in the twinkle of a hobby-horse.'

He also had '"Balsamum Stobule Swordum", or an oint-ment that's good against all cuts, green or canker'd wounds'. The pitch went on:

> Now suppose any honest man amongst you has hurt or cut himself with either sword, gun, or musket, spit, jack or grid-iron, glass bottle or pint pot; by the help and application of this my celebrated Balsam, they are immediately cur'd with-out giving themselves the trouble of sending for an illiterate surgeon, who will sooner cleanse their pockets of money than the wound of its infection.

Rand was not interested in taking people's money, naturally.

> Then gentlemen, see here is my 'Purando's Tankapon Tolos', that is to say in the Arabian language, the 'Wonderworking Pills', the excellent quality of which is hardly even known to myself. They purgeth the brain from all crassick, cloudifying humours, which obstruct the senses of all superannuated maids. They make the curratick directick and the directick indirectick in their lives and conversations. Then take three of these pills in the morning jejuno stomacho, with two quarts of aqua gruellis. I am none of those fellows that set an extravagant value upon themselves, merely because they ride upon spotted horses, but my medicines have made themselves and me famous throughout Asia, Africa, Europe and America.

He then went to boast of those he had cured. 'It was I, cur'd Prester John's Juggler's wife of a fistula in her elbow of which she died.' Not a very effective cure then.

> It was I, prevented the old woman from Exeter from running headlong into a wine-cellar. It was me, and only me, that cur'd the French Dancing Man in Amsterdam of consumption in his pocket. It was me who perform'd an excellent cure upon Captain Nonsuch, commander of the Nonnomen Galley, who had a cannon ball lodged in his little finger, likewise the carpenter of the same ship who had swallowed a handspike.

Through Rand was unashamedly a quack, he must have attracted customers or he would not have been in business. And perhaps his conman's cures were no worse than those of more legitimate practitioners.

Phoenix livers and mermaids' tongue

Dressed in a scarlet coat covered in gold braid and a cocked hat with a feather in it, Ben Willmore sold his remedies on Tower Hill. He would hold up a small bottle and say:

> Gentlemen and ladies, Behold this vial, which contains in its narrow bounds what the whole universe cannot purchase, if sold at its true value.

This admirable, this miraculous elixir, drawn from the hearts of mandrakes, phoenix livers, tongues of mermaids and distilled by contracted sunbeams, has, besides the unknown virtue of curing all distempers both of the mind and body, that divine one of animated the heart of man to that degree, that however remiss, cold and cowardly by nature, he shall become vigorous and brave.

Not only was his elixir a restorative, but also it could raise the dead:

> Gentlemen, if any of you present was at death's door, here's this, my Divine Elixir, will give you life again.
> This will recover whole fields of slain,
> And all the dead shall rise and fight again.

What self-respecting quack would be without a love potion? 'Here, gents, is my little paper of powder whose value surmounts that of rocks of diamonds and hills of gold. 'Twas this made Venus a goddess and gave her Apollo.'

He could hardly leave out the ladies.

Come, buy it ladies, you that would be fair and wear eternal youth, and you in whom the amorous fire remains when all the charms are fled; you that dress young and gay, that patch and paint, to fill up sometimes old furrows on your brows and set yourselves for conquest though in vain.

Here's that which will give you auburn hair, white teeth, red lips and dimples on your cheeks. Come, buy it, all you that are past bewitching, and you'd have handsome, young and active lovers.

Come all you City wives, that would advance your husbands to be Lord Mayors, come buy of me new beauty. This will give it, though now decayed as are your shop commodities; this will retrieve your customers and vend your false and out-of-fashion wares. Cheat, lye, protest and couzen [dupe] as you please, a handsome wife makes all a lawful gain.

There's more – it has aphrodisiac properties.

Here is my famous bottle of powder, the Life and Soul of Men. This is the Amorous Powder which Venus made and gave the god of love. 'Tis this alone that wounds and fires the heart, makes women kind and equals men to gods. 'Tis this that makes your great lady dote on the ill-favoured flop, your great man be jilted by this little mistress, your politician by his comedian, your chaplain by my lady's waiting women. In fine, sirs,
'Tis this, that cures the lover's pain
And Celia of her cold disdain.

I need say nothing of my Divine Baths of Reformation, nor the Wonders of the Old Oracle of the Box, which resolves all questions when sufficiently declared.

One can only imagine what the last two 'cures' might be.

The Irish stroker

The famous healer Valentine Greatrakes was known as the 'Irish stroker' because he cured his patients simply by massaging them. He wrote his own life story in a letter to the great scientist Robert Boyle, modestly entitled *A Brief Acccount of Mr Valentine Greatrakes and Divers of the Strange Cures by Him Lately Performed.* An account of his cures was published under the unassuming title *Wonders If Not Miracles* in 1666. It contains a number of testimonials from people who were cured or those who saw him cure people 'only by stroking'.

Mr Loyonell Beacher said that he saw Greatrakes 'stroke them, causing them to strip off their clothes'. They were 'persons of all ages and sex'. 'He stroked their breast with his hand and immediately the pain ceased.' Cripples threw away their crutches and the deaf could hear again when he put his finger in their ear.

One of the testimonials came from Eleanor Dickson, a 45-year-old widow from Clerkenwell, who could not get close to Greatrakes in Lincoln's Inn Field where he practised to be touched 'by reason of the throng'. Instead she obtained some of his urine, drank some and poured the rest in her ear. This, she said, cured her of the stomach troubles that had plagued her for years. As part of the process, four gallons of water and a great quantity of wind were voided from her 'privy part' and 'vomited out of her mouth several pieces of thick skin drawn over with blue veins like to a fresh bladder'. Her 72-inch waist shrank to 27 inches and her hearing was cured.

Not everyone was impressed. In a poem called 'Rub for Rub, or the Stroker Stroked', also published in 1666, the anonymous author claimed to have discovered the secret of Greatrakes's success with his women patients at least. He told of one young women taking her stockings off so that he can stroke: 'Her legs, her knees, her thighs, a little higher, And there's the doctor's centre of desire.' The poem continued:

One wench, I hear, and her diseases was this,
And that no strange one is, the green-sickness,
He saw the maid was in a needy mood,
He strait presum'd a clyster might be good:
He lays her on the bed, O beastly story!
And then thrusts in his long suppository,
And tells her on his faith, deny't who can,
Nothing so good for her as th'oyl of man.
And then I'm sure if what is true were spoke,
She gave him touch for touch, and stroke
    for stroke.
But passing this, and many o' th' like sort,
Doctor, your practice hath no good report;
And all suppose by your obscene narration,
Your brains and back want a severe purgation
Your pamphlet's false, reason itself implies,
For 'twas all poetry, and therefore lies.
Thus you and I upon the matter strike,
You give a rub, and I return the like.

This poem seems to have done the trick. Eventually the patients stopped coming and Greatrakes returned to Ireland, where he died in obscurity.

The hangman's remedy

As medical science developed, those who saw themselves as legitimate physicians sought to drive quacks out of business. One such was E. Gray, who was 'a doctor at physick, one of His late Majesties physicians, above 20 years since fellow of King's College in Cambridge, and now at the Golden Ball in Hatten-garden, near Holbourn', who published a handbill titled: 'A CAUTION TO THE UNWARY.' This drew the battle lines.

'Tis generally acknowledged throughout all Europe that no nation has been so fortunate in producing such eminent physicians as this kingdom of ours, and 'tis obvious to every eye that no country was ever pestered with so many ignorant quacks and empericks...

The word 'empericks' derives from the Greek *empirici*, who were members of a sect of ancient physicians who drew their techniques directly from experience rather than from philosophy or method.

...The enthusiasts in divinity, having no sooner acted his part and had his exit, but on the same stage, from his shop (or some worse place) enters the enthusiasts in physick; yesterday a taylor, heel-maker, barber, serving-man, rope-dancer, etc, to-day per saltum [in one leap], a learned doctor, able to instruct Aesculapius [the Roman god of medicine] himself, for he never obliged mankind yet with a panacea, a universal pill or powder, that could cure all diseases, which now every post can direct you to do, though it proves only the hangman's remedy for all diseases by death.

Pudet haec opprobria dici, for shame my dear countrymen, re-assume your reasons, and expose not your bodies and purses to the handling of such illiterate fellows, who never had the education of a grammar school, much less a university.

Nor be ye so irrational as to imagine anything extraordinary (unless it be ignorance) in a pair of outlandish whiskers, though he is so impudent to tell you, he had been physicians to three emperors and nine kings; when in his own country, he durst not give physick to a cobler.

Nor be ye gull'd with another sort of impostor, who allures you to him with 'cure without money', but when once he has got you into his clutches, he handles you so unmercifully as he does unskilfully.

Nor be ye imposed on by the pretence of any Herculean Medicine, that shall with four doses, at five shillings a dose, cure the most inveterate pox, a distemper not to be eradicated (in the opinion of the most learned in all the ages) with less than a renovation of all the humours in the whole body.

On the other hand, Gray was offering exactly the same thing as many he condemned were offering – 'the easiest and speediest ways of curing'.

Raising the dead

This last tale is not about England, nor does it involve an Englishman, but it demonstrates that the English are not uniquely gullible when it comes to quacks and it is such a good story that I could not leave it out.

An Italian quack named Mantacinni travelled around Europe in great style. He had a splendid coach and pair and was accompanied by a liveried servant. When he arrived in Lyons, he announced that he could raise the dead at will. To prove it, in 15 days time he said he would go to the graveyard and revive everyone who had been buried there in the last ten years. In the meantime, he asked the local magistrate to put him under guard, so that he could not abscond until he had fulfilled his promise.

Mantacinni's claim naturally attracted enormous interest and inflated his reputation. Intrigued, the Lyonnais flocked to his door and he cleaned up giving private consultations and

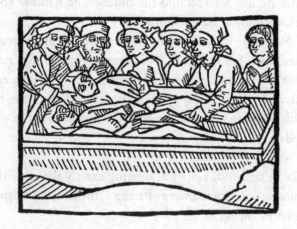

selling the unwary his '*Baume de Vie*', which he claimed prolonged life.

As the day of the promised resurrection approached, his servant grew afraid and told his master that he feared the consequences if he could not raise the dead in the graveyard as he had claimed.

'You know nothing of human nature,' Mantacinni told the servant. 'Just wait and be quiet.'

Soon after, a letter arrived. It was from a widower who had recently lost his wife.

'She was a harridan,' it said. 'I am unhappy enough without her resurrection.'

He pleaded with Mantacinni not to go ahead and offered him 50 louis to keep the secret of reviving the dead to himself. Then two young men called. They begged Mantacinni not to raise their father. He had been a miser and, if he were resurrected, he would rob them of their inheritance and reduce them to poverty again. A young widow, who was about to be married again, followed them. She begged Mantacinni not to raise her first husband. Again the miser's sons and the young widow were happy to pay the doctor good money not to resurrect their loved ones.

As the deadline drew near, the citizens of Lyons were near to panic. It seemed that nearly everyone had a reason for not wanting one or more of the inhabitants of the graveyard raised. Fearing a riot, with a day to go, the magistrate stepped in.

'I have no doubt that you will be able to resurrect the dead in the graveyard tomorrow,' he told Mantacinni. 'But the city is in uproar and I beg you not to attempt it, so that peace can be restored.'

Mantacinni was bribed to leave Lyons. He was given a document from the magistrate under the seal of the city, which certified that, with his 'rare and divine powers', Mantacinni could indeed raise the dead, but it was 'our fault that we were not eyewitness to your powers'. And he left the city with his pockets lined with gold.

Old England

How well Mantacinni would have done if he had crossed the Channel it is hard to say. With all the pills, potions and life-giving elixirs covered in this book, one would have thought that there would have been not one graveyard in England in the first place. However, despite all the curious cures of old England, people have mysteriously persisted in dying.